Practical
FLOWERING SHRUBS

Patrick Johns

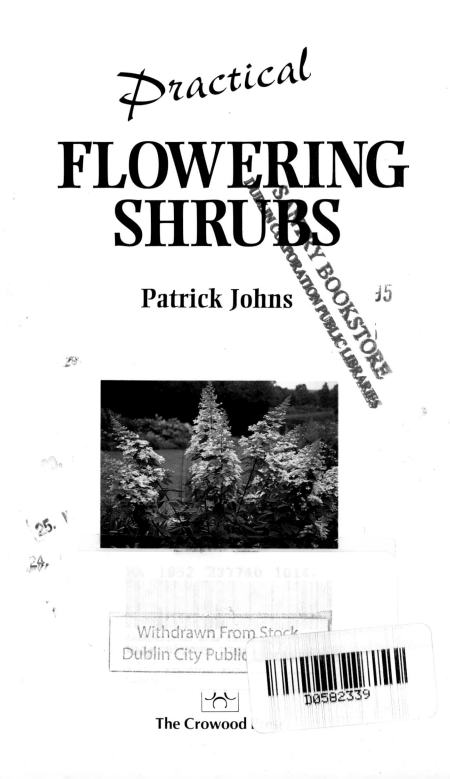

The Crowood

First published in 1993 by
The Crowood Press Ltd
Ramsbury, Marlborough
Wiltshire SN8 2HR

British Library Cataloguing-in-Publication Data

A catalogue record for this book is available from the British
Library.

ISBN 1 85223 774 0

Acknowledgements
Line-drawings by Claire Upsdale-Jones.
All photographs are by Dave Pike except those on pages 1,
2/3, 18, 20 (bottom), 28 (top), 31, 48, 55, 56 (top), 61 and 63
which are by Patrick Johns. Other photographs reproduced by
courtesy of Natural Image: pages 6 (bottom), 11, 17 (bottom),
23 (bottom), 32 and 45 by Robin Fletcher; page 23 (top) by
Bob Gibbons and page 17 (top) by Liz Gibbons. Front cover
photograph by Patrick Johns; back cover by Dave Pike.

Typeset in Optima by Chippendale Type Ltd,
Otley, West Yorkshire
Printed and bound in Great Britain by
BPCC Paulton Books Ltd

CONTENTS

INTRODUCTION

Flowering shrubs are grown for a number of different reasons, under a variety of climatic conditions and types of soil. They are ideally suited for modern gardens and yet they have been cultivated for many years; some were introduced around the time of the Norman Conquest and no doubt many were brought back by mariners and other travellers during the Dark Ages. With careful planning, a range of shrubs will provide interest throughout the year with comparatively little trouble; in fact, these woody plants require much less maintenance than many other types of plant that are often grown for decoration in the garden.

In addition to their blossom, shrubs can also provide a variety of form and leaf texture to add to their interest; fruit, coloured and variegated foliage, autumn tints and bark effect are other attributes.

Acer Palmatum *(Japanese Maple) is a superb specimen shrub, with its brightly coloured foliage in spring and autumn.*

Uses

A single isolated shrub can transform a monotonous area into a pleasing feature: perhaps a specimen growing in a container on a patio, or a number of specimens in combination forming a shrubbery. Many

Sambucus racemosus *'Sutherland' is one of the best foliage and fruiting shrubs.*

shrubs provide a useful living screen, for use either as a windbreak (much more efficient than a solid barrier), or to blot out an unsightly view. The prickly subjects are often very good to keep out animals — after all, farmers have been using shrubs for that purpose for centuries — but do take precautions to protect young children, and yourself, when tending the plants.

Some shrubs can be used for shelter, and to provide more congenial conditions for smaller, tender plants. They can be used in association with other subjects, sometimes in order to impart an atmosphere of maturity and permanence, but they must be allowed to retain their true habit free from restriction. This is where it is important to know their natural habit before they are planted, always bearing in mind the way in which a plant can complement, rather than compete with its neighbours.

Their value as ground-cover plants to suppress weed growth, to prevent unwanted 'short-cuts' across a lawn, or to prevent soil erosion on a sloping site make shrubs valuable under certain conditions. Ugly, but necessary contraptions such as a manhole cover can be camouflaged easily by planting a shrub alongside, especially one with prostrate growth, so that it grows over and yet is easily moved away when required.

Growth Forms

There is such a wide variety of shape and size available that shrubs can fit into virtually any scheme. Natural shapes are those which follow the form produced by a healthy plant growing unrestricted without being overshadowed, or tormented by a persistent prevailing wind.

There are, broadly speaking, five different shapes. The first is what might be termed the typical bush, or fan, represented by forms like the Butterfly bush (*Buddleia davidii*). Then there is the softly rounded, or 'bun' shape produced by, for example, *Genista lydia*. Next comes the narrow columnar upright, or fastigiate 'exclamation mark' shape as with *Viburnum fragrans*, useful to give height to a planting scheme consisting mainly of low-growing subjects. Weeping plants with pendant stems are interesting in their right place, such as the

Kilmarnock Willow (*Salix caprea 'Pendula'*) planted alongside a water feature. Horizontal shapes hugging the ground are useful to give added dimension; a typical plant to represent this shape is *Cotoneaster horizontalis*, and within this group we should add taller plants, but still with horizontal branches, such as *Viburnum tomentosum mariesii*.

A range of different sizes will be found within each shape group, and even the same species may vary to a certain extent in different locations for reasons of soil type, nutrition, aspect and climate. Size and shape can be modified by pruning so that we can add various other groups to the collection, such as the standard, a typical example being a standard rose. Different kinds of plant can be trained into fan shape, or espalier with tiered lateral stems one above the other growing from a central stem. The cascade lends itself to being planted on a terrace, so that its stems flow like a waterfall over the side. Some shapes, such as the ball, spiral and box, can be made by clipping.

Choisya ternata 'Sundance' is a golden-leaved evergreen with aromatic foliage, and sweetly scented flowers in spring.

Ceanothus repens is a first-class ground cover shrub, or can be used to cover a sheltered wall. The mid-blue flowers are borne from June to October.

1 • PLANNING AND PLANTING

Buying Plants

Numerous outlets are available for obtaining plants, from a market stall to large garden centre or nursery, with various other opportunities in between such as the plants on display at gardens open to the public; friends and neighbours can also be a good source. Television programmes, books and gardening club meetings prompt interest in specific shrubs, but a vast number of plants are purchased on impulse. An especially well-grown plant displayed with a mass of bloom is very tempting; unfortunately it does not always look so good after a short time in the garden. This may be due to a lack of knowledge of the plant's requirements. Regrettably the advice given at some retail establishments leaves something to be desired, although plant labels are now often reasonably informative and provide

Aucuba 'crotonifolia' *is extremely hardy, and does well in most soil types. Its bold, bright foliage is very attractive.*

Common name Sun rose
Botanical name *Helianthemum nummularium*
Hardiness rating Hardy
Care rating Easy
Description Evergreen good for ground cover. 1ft (30cm)
Peak interest Summer
Growth rate Fast
Soil needs Any soil; sunny position
Treatment Lightly trim straggly plants after flowering
Propagation Summer cuttings 1–2in (25–50mm) long

information regarding soil type and other cultural details.

Consideration should be given to the preferred soil type required for a particular plant – does it need an acid, or alkaline growing medium? What about moisture regime – will it tolerate prolonged dryness at the root? Some shrubs, for instance azaleas, will make a certain amount of shoot growth in moderately dry soil, but if the roots are too dry during mid-summer when the plant is thinking about initiating flower buds for the next spring, the display may be disappointing then. Some plants will be happy growing in shade, while others will flourish only in good light; hardiness is another very important aspect in the plant's welfare.

A point often overlooked concerns the toxicity of various parts of the plant. This is especially important if young children or pets enjoy the garden. In addition to berries, the leaves and sap of certain plants can at worst be lethal, or at least cause skin irritation. The health of the plant itself is important too, so do look for signs of attack by pest and disease; if either is evident, or if the plant looks unhealthy in any other way it is better not to take it; there is always another on offer, unless the plant is extremely rare.

The majority of shrubs are offered for sale in containers. Container-grown plants should be well established in the container. They are usually more expensive than 'bare-root' plants lifted from the field, but they can be transplanted at any time of the year. Some retailers simply dig up plants and pot them into containers for immediate sale and charge the same higher price for them. The root ball of plants grown in a container should remain in the pot when the plant is lifted by its stem; otherwise the container is likely to drop off together with the surrounding rooting medium (compost).

Although bare-root plants cost less than those of a similar age established in a container, there is more risk with them because the roots may have dried out severely between the time of lifting and your planting in the garden. Another disadvantage is that they can only be transplanted at certain times of the year — autumn and spring for evergreens and, after leaf fall, up to early spring for deciduous shrubs — soil conditions and weather permitting.

A ten point plan to detect a suspect plant:

1 Surface moss, lichen or weeds on growing medium.
2 Roots growing out of top or bottom of container.
3 Wilting leaves with parched container contents.

. The root ball of plants growing in a container should remain in the pot when the plant is lifted by its stem.

Roots growing out of the drainage holes in the base of a container suggest neglect and starvation.

4 Abnormal, spindly or straggly growth; trained specimens should be of good shape – that is what the extra cost is for!
5 Starved, weak stems with lower leaves missing or yellow when they should be green.
6 Wilting leaves with wet soil suggest a root disorder.
7 Broken stems and branches.
8 Variegated plant with reverted, green shoot (although this can usually be satisfactorily cut out).
9 Soft growth due to forcing.
10 Tender plants stood out for display without protection.

wrap it round with secure polythene sheeting. When you get the plant home, transplant it as soon as possible; otherwise protect it from blowing over if it is in a container.

One problem with bare-root plants is that they tend to dry out; once you get the plant home, the roots should be covered with soil or damp sacking to prevent them, and the stem, from drying out. The best way to achieve that is to dig a shallow trench, insert the roots so that the plant is at an angle to prevent wind rock, then cover the roots. Sometimes plants are enclosed in

Unless planting can take place straight away, the roots should be protected from drying out. One method is to heel them in at an angle to prevent wind-rock.

Plants with variegated leaves sometimes produce a shoot with entirely green leaves. These reverted shoots should be cut out.

If the chosen plant is satisfactory in all respects and you can afford it (some look very expensive), do not be put off by price: think of it in terms of investment in enjoyment and divide the cost by its expected life-span!

Unless it is a leafless, deciduous plant, take delivery in a covered vehicle; the chill factor in an open-backed lorry or on the roof-rack of a car could risk its survival. If the plant can only be transported in that way, cover it with a plastic bin-liner, or

straw or some other material for despatch during winter. In addition to conserving moisture, the plant is protected from frost and mechanical damage. The material should be removed as soon as possible, otherwise fungal diseases may be encouraged to attack the plant.

Roots found to be dry on unpacking can sometimes be revived when they are soaked in a container of water. However, that should be avoided whenever possible and only used as a last resort because plants given such treatment do not usually establish well after planting.

Site and Aspect

Some plants tolerate and some even desire shade, but the position should not be too shaded. Nor should it be subject to strong wind, although some shrubs can withstand a certain amount of buffeting and can be grown as a windbreak. While many plants enjoy full sun, there are others, such as gold-foliaged subjects, which prefer dappled shade, or at least to be out of the strong rays of the midday sun. Some plants, although normally hardy, are susceptible to frost damage at certain times. Camellias, for example, are hardy but their flowers are inclined to be scorched by frost thawing quickly when the sun shines on them early in the morning; frost pockets should therefore be avoided for such plants. These and similar spring-flowering plants would be better planted in a site other than one facing east.

Gardens vary enormously in their microclimate: plants that flourish in one garden may put on very inferior growth, or perhaps not grow at all on a site less than a mile away. The reasons for this vary in that soil

The popular Potentilla fruticosa, *with its bright yellow flowers, is best in full sun.*

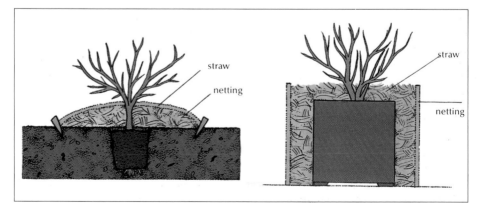

Frost protection. A layer of straw held down with netting will help to protect the roots of frost-sensitive species, such as camellias and magnolias during their first winter.
Straw completely surrounding the roots of container shrubs, again held in place with netting, gives essential frost protection during the cold months.

types are inclined to change dramatically in some areas, from acid sands to alkaline loam. Other things being equal, mature gardens with overshadowing trees that restrict the entry of sun are likely to benefit some plants, yet be detrimental to others which would flourish in a garden with more sunlight. With factors such as this in mind, it is not always advisable to select plants which generally perform well in the local neighbourhood, although the area could provide some useful pointers.

While walls and hedges can provide shelter, they can also cause a frost pocket where one would not normally develop, especially on a sloping site. Frosty air is heavy and is inclined to roll down a slope, tending to build up at the bottom; thus any susceptible plants below the frost line are liable to be damaged. One way to avoid such a problem is to cut drainage holes in the base of the obstruction so that the heavy frost-laden air is allowed to pass on down the slope.

Hedges of mixed shrubs can provide an attractive feature if properly maintained. Here honeysuckle and berberis are combined.

Walls and hedges can provide shelter but they can also create a frost pocket.

A southerly aspect, or one facing west is normally warmer than those facing east or north. A site facing south is the warmest of all since it reaps the benefit of a longer duration of sun, especially in winter, and it is also in the full range of the midday sun.

An easterly aspect gains the benefit of early morning sun but this, at least in winter and early spring, coincides with air still chilled by a cold night and so takes a long time to warm up; by then the sun may well have moved on. A west-facing site can also be limited in the amount of direct sunlight it receives, although it can be very useful for those subjects which flower in early spring. The aspect facing north is usually the coldest with the least amount of sun. Fortunately, there is a range of plants suited to any of these positions and so even the coldest of gardens need not be at a loss for interest, although a more congenial site is likely to give more pleasure.

Containers

Plants growing in containers have the advantage in that they can be moved around and tender subjects can even be taken into more favourable conditions during winter. Containers often provide the opportunity to give prominence to

One of the most popular climbers, wisteria's beautiful flowers hang in pendulous racemes during May and June. It needs a sunny sheltered site, with well-drained fertile soil.

specimens with a definite seasonal interest, so that they can be replaced by others as necessary, then moved back when they are at their best again. Container growing provides the chance to grow plants in an otherwise difficult situation, for example, where the ground is unworkable for one reason or another, possibly due to a covering of paving in a courtyard. There is often a desire to grow plants which would not thrive in a particular garden soil – here again, a container gives scope to create the conditions necessary by filling it with suitable growing medium.

Containers made from a wide range of materials are available and some care is needed in their selection. Cost may well be a deciding factor, but it pays to buy the best quality that one can afford because a well-made, attractive container can do much to improve the feature. Terracotta is an all-time favourite and the material can withstand a considerable amount of frost,

provided it is well fired. However, there are products on offer which, when subjected to

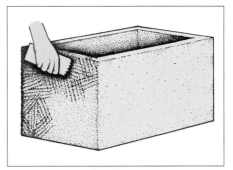

Containers made in smooth-sided moulds often need to be worked if they are to resemble old stone vessels. This is best done using a flat piece of wood to smooth any sharp edges, while a flat piece of boxwood with 'teeth' cut into it makes a useful comb to roughen the sides.

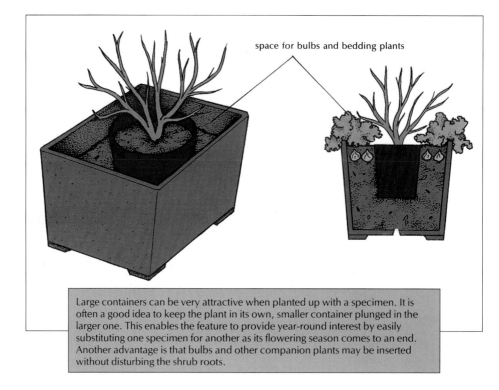

space for bulbs and bedding plants

Large containers can be very attractive when planted up with a specimen. It is often a good idea to keep the plant in its own, smaller container plunged in the larger one. This enables the feature to provide year-round interest by easily substituting one specimen for another as its flowering season comes to an end. Another advantage is that bulbs and other companion plants may be inserted without disturbing the shrub roots.

low temperatures, tend to crack and flake. Even so, the best terracotta can be susceptible to cracking when the contents expand on freezing, and so precautions should be taken in winter by standing the container on small blocks so that excess water can drain away.

It is worth soaking clay containers in clear water for a few hours before use. This will remove salts from the material, which would otherwise slowly collect on the surface later. The inside surface of the container should then be allowed to dry before filling so that the root ball will come away cleanly when the time comes to move the plant into a larger container.

Various other materials can be used to make containers, including concrete. This tends to be rather heavy but is usually strong and some of the more expensive products are attractive. Soaking in clear water is advisable to remove some of the alkalinity, especially when it is intended for an ericaceous plant. Plastics are less costly, and tough but light to handle; they usually demand less watering when the contained plant is small since evaporation from the wall does not take place, although there is virtually no difference in water requirement when the plant is large because the major water loss then is through the leaf surface.

Wooden barrels make interesting containers, especially the small whisky pattern available at most garden centres. The home handyman can also make good use of wood to make various shapes.

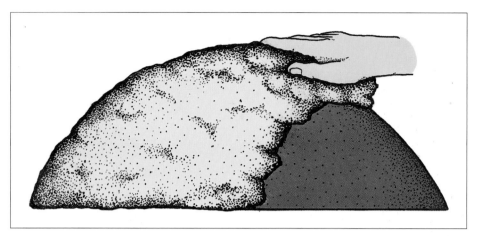

Containers of all shapes and sizes can be made from hypertufa. Make a mould from a heap of moist compacted sand, and press the small lumps of hypertufa together to form the desired shape. The container can be made even stronger by inserting galvanised wire netting while the hypertufa is being applied. Cut small drainage holes in the base when the mixture begins to set.

Whichever kind of material is selected, it should be remembered that plants dislike being waterlogged and so provision must always be provided for adequate drainage at the base. Old-fashioned hydrangea vessels have drainage holes, not in the base, but on the side close to the bottom so that worms are less likely to enter the

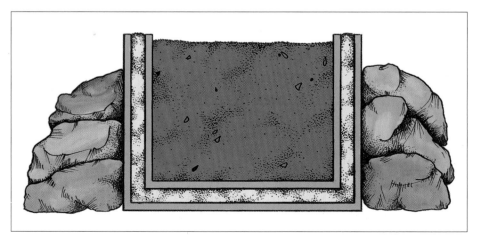

Cardboard boxes can be used to form a mould; the larger box being supported at the sides with rocks and the inner box with compressed soil. Rip away the cardboard after a few days when the hypertufa is perfectly hard.

container and disturb the roots. Another way to prevent pests gaining entry is to place a small piece of plastic gauze inside the container over the drainage hole.

Bear in mind that if a plant will need to be moved on into a larger container sometime in the future, it will have to be removed from the existing one. The shape of the container is therefore important so that the root ball will move out easily. Another point to remember is that plant diseases may be lurking in previously used containers and so it is advisable to wash it out thoroughly – in any case, the interior needs to be clean to prevent the roots from clinging to the sides.

Take care with the kind of planting medium (often incorrectly called 'compost') that you use for the container. In the first place, certain plants will not tolerate an alkaline medium, and others do not thrive when the growing conditions are acid. The most suitable medium for the majority of shrubs is a mixture of loam, peat, sand and fertilizer, including lime for those subjects that like it. Similar mixes without lime are available for lime-hating plants. These soil-based mixtures are much easier to maintain than soilless media because the soil gives them more buffering against over-feeding, for example; provided they have the correct ingredients, they are less likely to be over-watered and they tend to keep their structure longer. Suitable mixtures are available at garden centres and other garden supply outlets.

Soilless media such as peat or processed bark are inclined to lose their nutrient value after a comparatively short space of time and although the major plant foods are easily rectified, certain minor (trace) elements are more difficult to monitor. Having said that, plants grown in containers commercially are usually in loamless media because they are likely to be in their containers for a comparatively short time, the medium does not need sterilizing as would

soil, and it is lighter and therefore easier to handle.

Whichever kind of medium is used, drainage is of paramount importance and so, once the gauze is in place, a layer of pebbles, shingle, polystyrene or other freely draining material is put into the container. Next, put in sufficient growing medium so that when it is firmed down and the root ball is offered in, there is sufficient space between the surface of the roots and the rim of the container to allow for watering. This space will vary according to the size of the container but should be no less than an inch (25mm), and more if the surface is intended to be mulched with pebbles or chipped bark.

Having made sure that the root ball is moist by previously watering and allowing to drain, remove the plant from the existing

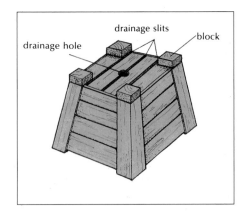

Containers need good drainage, and should be raised slightly off the ground.

container and place the root ball in the centre of its new home; take care not to dislodge any of the roots, otherwise the plant may suffer more of a check to growth than it deserves. Carefully fill in around the root ball with fresh medium, lightly firming as you go. Finally, give the container contents a good watering to ensure that the medium is uniformly moist throughout. It should be noted from the outset that a large container filled with loam-based medium can be very heavy, and so the work should, when possible, be carried out where the container is to stand.

An alternative to permanent planting is to keep the plant in its existing container and simply plunge into a larger one filled with peat, processed bark, coir or other material. This method lends itself to comparatively short-lived plants, or possibly to those of differing vigour.

Planning

It is the easiest thing in the world to plan a shrub feature – well almost! You simply plan whatever would give you most pleasure and not clutter your thoughts with grand ideas about vistas, surprises and the like – unless of course, you wish to incorporate such things. That is not to say that composition should be ignored, because form, texture and colour is important. The complete project should be considered with all of the specimens together so that the total effect is pleasing, but does not obscure the attractive features of the individual.

A hasty planting would not be the first project to be lifted and transplanted elsewhere! Before setting spade into soil it really is important to sit down and consider the garden as a whole, bearing in mind that once planted and given the correct treatment, a shrub can remain healthy for twenty years or more. Any collection of shrubs should harmonize with other features of the garden. Visualize the garden from more than one viewpoint. A specimen shrub may be an isolated feature in a lawn or on the patio, or several plants may be set out to form a shrub border. In that case, it

Garden ornaments are set off well against a background of a fine display of flowering shrubs.

Syringa (lilac) is usually grown for its scented flowers, but may be too large for smaller gardens.

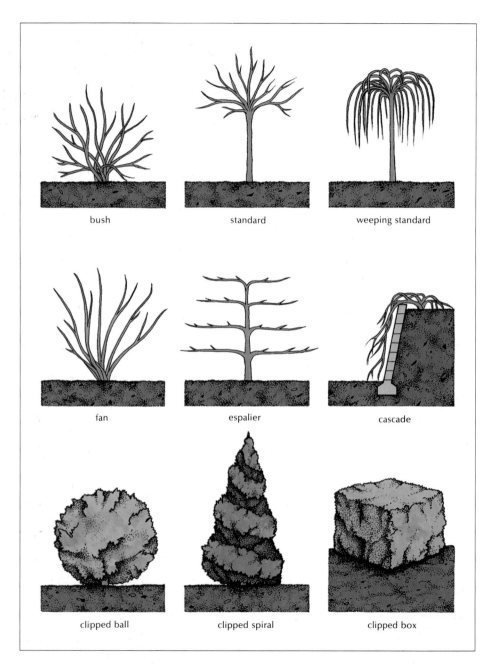

bush

standard

weeping standard

fan

espalier

cascade

clipped ball

clipped spiral

clipped box

Trained shrub forms.

is beneficial to have smaller plants in groups, with larger plants at the rear and also coming to the front to enhance the scheme. Too many different kinds of plant in a confined space lead to a restless effect; it is far more satisfying to plant three of a kind in a group so that they will eventually form an impressive feature, effectively one large bush. Avoid overcrowding: it is very easy to let enthusiasm run away at the expense of good planning – and the pocket!

Abelia grandiflora *has attractive pink and white flowers in summer. Grown against a sheltered wall in mild climates, it remains evergreen.*

It is not easy to anticipate how long it will take for a collection of plants to mature, and yet it is useful to have some idea of the vigour of each specimen; they are all likely to mature at different times and much depends on, for example, the soil climate. The plant will use the first year after planting to get established and so little growth may be seen, with the possibility that no flowers will appear, although well-grown specimens raised in containers are likely to perform well. The second year should see a good deal of action, especially if the plant has been well cared for regarding fertilizer and moisture at the root. Some of the more vigorous plants will be as large as required after the third year, while the slow-growing kinds will still have a long way to go. A good compromise in a new planting scheme would be to plant up the really permanent shrubs at their correct spacing – which may seem very generous at the time – so that they have sufficient room when they are full grown – and fill in with less expensive, faster growers which can be removed later as necessary.

Answers need to be found to questions

Common name   none
Botanical name   *Perovskia atriplicifolia*
Hardiness rating   Hardy
Care rating   Easy
Description   Deciduous; leaves have pleasant fragrance. 4ft (1.2m)
Peak interest   Summer
Growth rate   Fast
Soil needs   Any well-drained soil in full sun
Treatment   Cut back old stems in spring
Propagation   Semi-ripe cuttings late summer

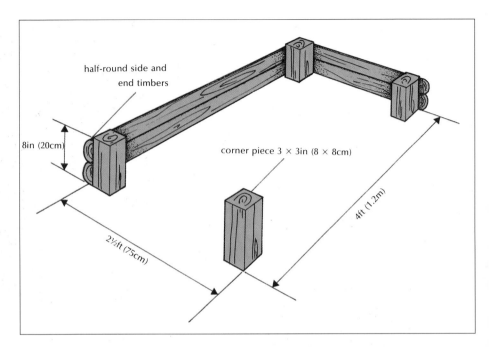

half-round side and
end timbers

8in (20cm)

corner piece 3 × 3in (8 × 8cm)

4ft (1.2m)

2½ft (75cm)

Raised bed construction. Bolt half-round timbers to uprights sunk into the ground. Fork up the base, and fill with topsoil. To make a peat bed, line the base with a plastic sheet then fill with a lime-free peat-based soil.

The flower fragrance is an added bonus with deciduous azaleas.

Flowers and foliage make Weigela florida variegata a worthwhile plant for any border.

regarding the amount of space to be given to shrubs; whether the plants are to form a mixed border with other decorative subjects, or to be on their own. The eventual height and spread of each plant is important so that they are given a reasonable amount of room to perform well. Site and aspect has already been discussed and that should be considered, together with the soil type most suited to the plant in question.

Elaeagnus pungens maculata *makes an interesting specimen shrub, or can be used for hedging.*

Evergreen shrubs are useful for providing year-round interest in the garden.

Remember that where space permits, a variety of shrubs can be selected to provide interest all year round, not only when they are in flower as some have interesting bark, foliage and/or fruit; leafless deciduous shrubs can look attractive even in winter when their shape is emphasized by frost. The leafless stems of willows and dogwoods can be encouraged to produce outstanding rind colours for winter decoration (*see* page 38).

Consideration should always be given to

evergreen plants so that the border has a furnished appearance at all times. A bright variegated-leaf evergreen such as *Elaeagnus pungens maculata* placed in a suitable position, perhaps so that it can be viewed from a living-room window, will be an impressive feature on a winter's day. Evergreens also provide a good backdrop for deciduous winter and early spring-flowering shrubs. Leaf texture is sometimes overlooked and yet a stroll around a large garden centre will show the great variety of shapes and sizes on offer. Plant form is also important, not only for its ongoing appearance, but plants with an attractive outline are good to see when they are in, or out of bloom.

In certain cases, a shrub border consisting of one species is most attractive. Given the correct soil conditions, a border of deciduous azaleas in springtime is difficult

to outshine. The only problem with these 'self' beds is that the period of paramount interest may be limited to a comparatively short time each year.

Not least of all, many shrubs attract butterflies and birds to add extra interest in the garden.

Planting

The soil should be in good heart to give the plants a good start. It always pays to prepare the ground properly before planting. Double digging is traditional but it is laborious because the second spade depth, as well as the first, is dug over. However, some soils, especially those with a thin layer of topsoil over sand or chalk, are best dug shallowly with, perhaps, the second spit forked over

Shrubs are available in a wide range of colours and textures.

Buddleia davidii *is an excellent shrub for attracting butterflies into the garden.*

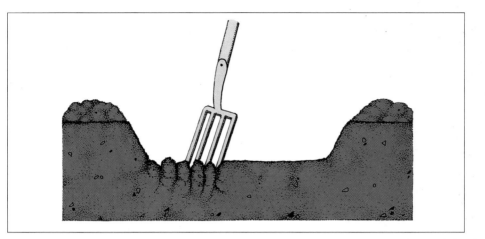

Poor drainage is often the result of a hard subsoil 'pan' caused by a layer of compacted soil or rock. If this is the case, dig down and break up the pan with a digging fork or crow bar. Otherwise a drainage system will need to be installed.

to break up any hard pan which would otherwise impede drainage. In addition to improving drainage, the purpose of digging is to incorporate bulky organic material such as garden compost, leafmould, etc., and to remove weeds and other debris. Digging will also help to create a good crumb structure and tilth.

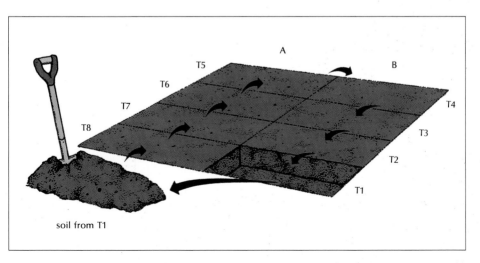

Double digging. Divide the bed into two halves A and B. Dig out a trench (T1) 10in (25cm) deep and place this soil by T8. Fork up the bottom of T1. Repeat the process as illustrated, filling T8 with the soil from T1.

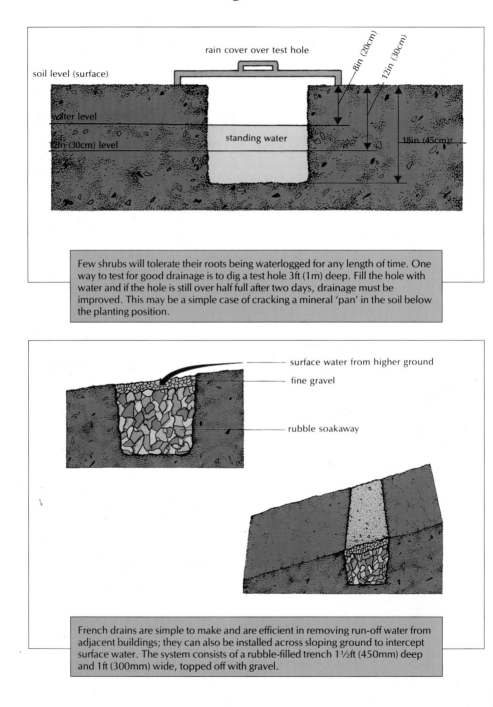

rain cover over test hole

soil level (surface)

8in (20cm)

12in (30cm)

water level

standing water

18in (45cm)

(30cm) level

Few shrubs will tolerate their roots being waterlogged for any length of time. One way to test for good drainage is to dig a test hole 3ft (1m) deep. Fill the hole with water and if the hole is still over half full after two days, drainage must be improved. This may be a simple case of cracking a mineral 'pan' in the soil below the planting position.

surface water from higher ground

fine gravel

rubble soakaway

French drains are simple to make and are efficient in removing run-off water from adjacent buildings; they can also be installed across sloping ground to intercept surface water. The system consists of a rubble-filled trench 1½ft (450mm) deep and 1ft (300mm) wide, topped off with gravel.

Heavy clay soil should be dug over before it becomes too wet in the autumn, then left rough for winter frost to break down the lumps. Digging such soil in late spring or summer results in the soil becoming more difficult to break down as the season progresses. Light, sandy soil is best dug over during spring, otherwise it may pan down on the surface following autumn and winter rain.

Some idea of the nutrient status and pH level of the soil should be determined before planting. Certain plants, for instance rhododendrons and azaleas, will not tolerate alkaline soil, while others are quite happy, indeed require such conditions to make healthy growth. Simple kits for testing the soil are available at garden

Common name   Rose of Sharon
Botanical name   *Hypericum calycinum*
Hardiness rating   Slightly tender; regrowth usual after hard frost
Care rating   Easy
Description   Evergreen and good for ground cover. 1ft (30cm)
Peak interest   Summer
Growth rate   Fast
Soil needs   Well-drained soil in sun or semi-shade
Treatment   Clip back straggly and frosted stems in spring
Propagation   Sow seed in spring; division of plants in spring

Common name   Lacecap Hydrangea
Botanical name   *Hydrangea macrophylla* 'Bluewave'
Hardiness rating   Fairly hardy
Care rating   Easy but care with deadheading
Description   Deciduous shrub producing pink flowers in some soils. 4½ft (1.4m)
Peak interest   Summer
Growth rate   Medium
Soil needs   Well-drained, acid soil in sun or semi-shade
Treatment   Remove spent flower heads by cutting back to fat bud below. Aluminium sulphate in soil will encourage blue flowers
Propagation   3–4in (75–100mm) long cuttings late summer

centres and other retailers, so there is no excuse for not creating desirable conditions for the plants. When liming is necessary it should, ideally, be carried out some weeks before planting so that the required chemical reaction will take place. Lime should never be applied at the same time as fertilizers or bulky organic material such as farmyard manure, for this will lead to rapid loss of plant foods. The actual amount of lime to be applied, if any, can be determined by following the instructions enclosed with the kit; label instructions on containers will indicate how much fertilizer should be given.

Avoid cultivating the soil when it is frozen or very wet, otherwise the texture will deteriorate and, in any case, the work is far more enjoyable under more favourable conditions.

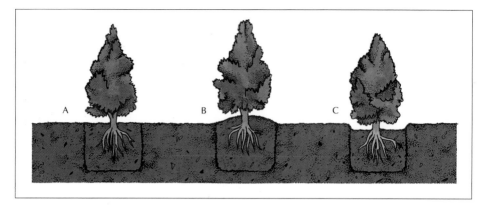

Planting depth. (a) on average soils, plants should be set at soil depth; (b) on heavy wet soils, plants should be slightly raised; (c) on dry sandy soils, plants should be set in a slight hollow.

When single specimens are planted in a lawn it will not, of course, be necessary to dig over an area much larger than the diameter of the root system. In any case, it will be necessary to dig out a hole sufficiently large to accommodate the roots without buckling; the best way to assess the diameter of the hole is to place the plant for a moment on the ground where it is to go before digging the hole. The hole should be sufficiently deep so that when the plant is inserted, the roots are at the same depth as they were before the plant was lifted from the nursery. The roots of containerized plants should finish at the same level as they are in the container.

Unless it has already been incorporated when digging, a forkful of garden compost, leafmould, processed bark or farmyard manure should be forked into the base of the hole. This will help to retain soil moisture and provide suitable conditions for the plant. It is important to avoid leaving a wad of the material in the hole, otherwise it may act as a sump and waterlog the roots. A sprinkling of fertilizer can be added to the hole and forked in at the same time.

Although cold (not frosty) winds will not

Dished soil. This assists watering in hot, dry conditions by preventing run-off.

be detrimental, exposure to drying winds will be. If it is necessary to keep bare-root plants (plants dug up from the soil to be transplanted) out of the ground for any length of time, they should be protected by covering the roots with sacking or weighted-down polythene sheet.

Place the root system, well spread out, centrally in the hole after firming the soil in the base. The hole is then gradually filled

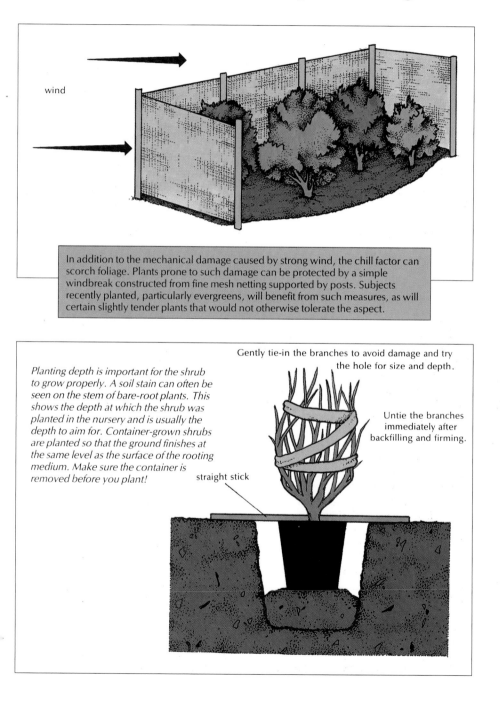

wind

In addition to the mechanical damage caused by strong wind, the chill factor can scorch foliage. Plants prone to such damage can be protected by a simple windbreak constructed from fine mesh netting supported by posts. Subjects recently planted, particularly evergreens, will benefit from such measures, as will certain slightly tender plants that would not otherwise tolerate the aspect.

Planting depth is important for the shrub to grow properly. A soil stain can often be seen on the stem of bare-root plants. This shows the depth at which the shrub was planted in the nursery and is usually the depth to aim for. Container-grown shrubs are planted so that the ground finishes at the same level as the surface of the rooting medium. Make sure the container is removed before you plant!

Gently tie-in the branches to avoid damage and try the hole for size and depth.

Untie the branches immediately after backfilling and firming.

straight stick

with soil so that it trickles between the roots, helped by carefully lifting the plant slightly up and down. Firm planting is essential and is best done by treading the heel in around the plant, taking care to avoid damaging the roots and shoots. See that the plant is at the correct depth by checking the soil mark on the stem. All that remains is to rake the soil surface level and, if at all dry, give the soil around the plant a thorough soaking with water. A surface mulch of bulky organic material will help to conserve moisture during the following spring. It should, ideally, be applied in late spring when the ground is moist.

Shrubs do not normally require stake supports unless they are poorly rooted and liable to be blown over, or when a standard is planted, in which case the stake should be driven into the hole before the roots are in place. This will avoid harming the roots (they will very likely be damaged if the stake is inserted after the plant is set out). When a stake is used, the plant should be secured by two ties, but do check them during the growing season to ensure they are not too tight. Plastic ties are available which hold no risk of strangling the plant.

Since containerized plants do not suffer root disturbance, they can be planted at any time of the year provided the soil is workable. Bare-root plants are set out during the

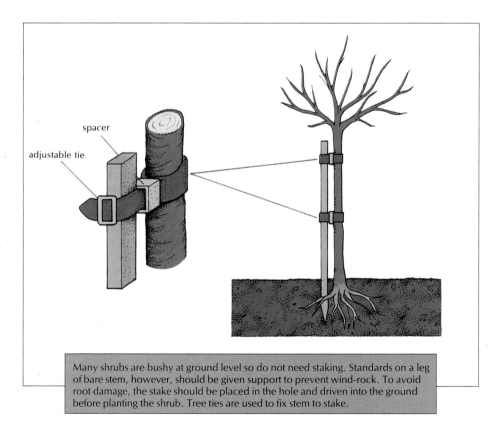

spacer

adjustable tie

Many shrubs are bushy at ground level so do not need staking. Standards on a leg of bare stem, however, should be given support to prevent wind-rock. To avoid root damage, the stake should be placed in the hole and driven into the ground before planting the shrub. Tree ties are used to fix stem to stake.

early autumn or spring for evergreens; from leaf fall through winter to spring – but preferably in autumn because they establish faster – for deciduous kinds. A mild, moist spell is ideal, such as often occurs in November and occasionally December. Bearing this in mind, the disturbed ground around the plants should be checked from time to time and refirmed if frost occurs later.

Evergreens are liable to lose some, if not all, of their leaves during the first winter after planting. That should not necessarily cause alarm, since it is nature's way of protecting the plant against excessive loss of moisture through transpiration. Large evergreen shrubs often benefit from having long stems reduced by cutting them back by half at planting time. This helps to reduce transpiration and the strain on the roots. The damage caused by cold, drying winds can be reduced by protecting evergreens with a screen made from netting.

One or two other points should be noted when dealing with containerized plants. Firstly, it is important to ensure that the root ball is moist before planting takes place; secondly, it is vital that the soil surrounding the root ball is firmed properly after planting so that shrinkage does not occur; and finally, make sure that you do not introduce weeds such as oxalis, thistle, bindweed and other difficult to eradicate plants with the contents of the container. Pests, for example, the larvae of vine weevils may also be present: notches eaten out of the leaf margins are a certain sign that all is not well in that respect.

In passing, it is worth making the point that the container must be removed when planting containerized plants. Some bare-root plants are lifted from the ground at the nursery and then 'balled' in sacking to prevent the soil from falling away in transit. It is important to remove the sacking at planting time. Although that may seem obvious, it has been known for plants

Transition soil. Shrubs raised in peat-based compost will establish faster if a soil/peat/sand transition mixture is used for backfilling the planting hole, instead of ordinary garden soil.

to perish through being planted in their original container!

Do make a note of the correct name for the plant; it makes the plant that much more interesting and, in any case, sooner or later someone is bound to ask what it is called. The name label supplied with the plant at the time of purchase is unlikely to last very long and so it is worth fixing a permanent label to the plant; various kinds are available. Zinc, aluminium and engraved labels tend to last longer than wood, paper and thin plastic ones. The latter become brittle and snap in a comparatively short space of time.

Transplanting

Plants propagated at home will need to be transplanted from time to time, as will those given as presents and lifted from the gardens of friends and neighbours. Hopefully it will not be necessary to move an incorrectly placed plant within one's own garden, although that does happen sometimes for one reason or another.

Much, if not all that has already been said under the heading of 'Planting' applies here (*see* page 20). Additionally, the pre-transplanting period should be given consideration. It is important to encourage the plant to get into the optimum state for its move, which can be a major operation. Established plants in containers should present no problem and they have a good chance of quickly becoming established since there is, or should be, no root disturbance. Bare-root plants, on the other hand, are liable to receive a nasty check to growth if too many of the roots are damaged to maintain the plant properly after lifting.

Common name   Darwin's Barberry
Botanical name   *Berberis darwinii*
Hardiness rating   Hardy
Care rating   Easy
Description   Evergreen with small prickly leaves. 8ft (2.4m)
Peak interest   Flowers spring; fruit summer
Growth rate   Medium
Soil needs   Any well-drained soil in sun or partial shade
Treatment   Prune congested old wood in spring
Propagation   Hardwood 5–7in (125–175mm) late autumn/early winter

Garrya elliptica is a hardy plant providing interest during the dark days of winter.

Whenever possible, transplanting should be anticipated one year ahead by cutting around the roots with a spade. This is achieved simply by inserting the spade vertically into the ground around the root zone some distance away from the stems. The actual distance will depend on the size of the plant but the area just inside and below the overhang of topgrowth should be right. The idea of this root severance is to encourage the plant to produce more lateral roots during the following growing season; the ball of roots will then contain more actively-growing fibrous roots to support the plant after lifting.

Have sacking, or a sheet of strong polythene handy for when the plant is dug from the ground. Once lifted, the shrub, together with as much soil adhering to the roots as possible, is placed on the sheet. A small plant will probably be light so it can be carried to its new location, or at least lifted into a wheelbarrow; large plants together with their root ball, however, are likely to be too heavy to carry far and so they can be dragged along on the sheet.

All that remains to do is to prepare the planting hole and set in the plant as already outlined above, but do avoid working the soil when it is wet, otherwise the roots are likely to suffocate.

2 • CULTIVATION AND CARE

Watering

Water is important for the plant in many ways; after all, over 90 per cent of the plant consists of water. It is necessary for the transport of soluble nutrients taken up by the roots, and to move food around within the plant; it is an important factor in photosynthesis when the plant utilizes light with carbon dioxide and water to manufacture its food; water keeps the plant turgid, and also helps to keep it cool when necessary. Therefore, when the plant is short of water at the roots it is in a static state, and if the dryness is prolonged it could even die. Conversely, if the soil is too wet and waterlogged, the plant would not thrive due to insufficient air around the roots.

A simple moisture meter which you push down into the soil will save your plants from being over-watered and tell you if the soil is too dry.

Common name   Mexican Orange Blossom
Botanical name   *Choisya ternata*
Hardiness rating   Protect from strong wind and hard frost
Care rating   Easy
Description   Pungent evergreen leaves when crushed; fragrant flowers. 9ft (2.7m)
Peak interest   Spring but often flowers until autumn frost
Growth rate   Fast
Soil needs   Any well-drained soil in sunny position
Treatment   Trim to shape after flowering
Propagation   Cuttings 2–3in (50–75mm) long in summer, or 4–6in (100–150mm) long in autumn

Various gadgets are available to place in the soil to see whether irrigation is necessary, but even without the use of a device it is easy to see when irrigation is required. The simplest method is to squeeze a handful of soil in the palm of the hand; if this results in moisture oozing between the fingers, then the soil is likely to be sufficiently moist – possibly too wet. When the soil binds together without releasing a visible amount of moisture and then shatters when it is dropped to the ground, it is probably just right. The ideal level to check is at root depth, and a soil auger is useful for taking samples at various depths. This implement resembles a large corkscrew and can be made out of a wood-boring auger. The idea is to screw the auger into the ground, then withdraw it without twisting it so that the soil remains in the groove. The soil is then removed and given the squeeze test.

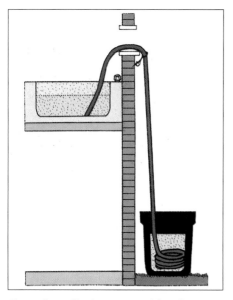

Plants often suffer during times of drought – especially when a hose-pipe ban is in force. One alternative is the use of bath water, but avoid using bath salts, oil or foam.

Irrigation is best considered in various phases. Phase one is at planting time when the soil should be moist without being too wet. Plants will not establish properly in dust-dry soil. Any watering that is necessary at that stage should be carried out well before digging the hole so that the soil will moisten thoroughly and have enough time for any surplus water to drain away. The second stage is when the plant is watered in immediately after planting, when water is applied to the soil surface over the root zone. The third stage is when the plant is becoming established during the first summer after planting; it is essential to keep the root zone moist then. The final stage is during the active season of growth for the remainder of its life. This is particularly important for those plants which flower during spring because they initiate their flower buds in the preceding summer, a time when they are likely to be short of

Various sprinklers are available for watering shrubs. They are usually manually controlled, although some can be automated.

water. If that does happen they will probably have a year without flowering – camellias and azaleas are particularly prone to this problem.

It is important to moisten the root system thoroughly, when irrigation is applied. Tiny dribbles are worse than useless because they tend to encourage roots to grow at the surface where they are more likely to be susceptible to subsequent drought. Try to water in the evening, as there is less wastage through evaporation then. Even so, a considerable wastage takes place when the water is applied by overhead sprayline. Wastage also occurs when water is applied directly from the end of a hose, since more goes to drainage than when the same volume is applied gradually, for example, by means of a rose on the end of a hose. The best form of irrigation equipment is underground tube, perforated to allow the water to seep through; it could be placed below the surface mulch. Alternatively, perforated layflat polythene tubing could be laid on the surface of the soil, with one end closed up and the other fixed to the water source. The tubing is sufficiently flexible for it to wander serpentine-like among the plants.

Try to anticipate the need for watering to prevent the leaves wilting. Also, avoid wetting the leaves in strong sunshine otherwise leaf scorch may result from the sun shining through water droplets which act like a magnifying glass. If any water is needed, do apply it before a surface mulch, for the mulch, particularly if it is dry, may act as an umbrella and shed water away from the root zone.

There is a greater need for watering a container-grown shrub than one growing in the open ground, since the roots are confined. However, it is easy to establish whether water is required, especially for plants growing in terracotta which tends to give a ringing sound when tapped with a pebble or other solid object. When the

Common name none
Botanical name *Cotoneaster conspicuus* 'Decorus'
Hardiness rating Hardy
Care rating Easy
Description Ground-hugging evergreen; can be trained as weeping standard. 2½ft (0.75m)
Peak interest Summer flowers; winter berries
Growth rate Medium
Soil needs Any well-drained soil in full sun
Treatment Cut out upward-growing shoots
Propagation Summer cuttings 3–5in (75–125mm) long

contents are moist, a dull thud can be heard. Other types of container, such as wood or fibre, do not give this message and so other means must be employed. Experienced gardeners are often able to see from the colour or tell from the feel of the growing medium whether irrigation is necessary; the less experienced may resort to one of the moisture meters available, or a detection stick. This aid resembles a plant label and is pushed into the root zone; as it dries out, the stick changes colour.

Active shrubs take up a good deal of water during summer. It may be necessary to water an established shrub with its container full of roots twice daily during hot weather. If the root ball does dry out and shrink away from the container, it may be necessary to dunk the container, root ball and all, into a larger vessel of water. Leave it there until bubbles cease to rise to the surface, then stand it out to drain. This should rarely, if ever, be necessary when a gap has been left at the top of the growing container sufficiently large to take enough water to moisten the roots thoroughly.

Keep an eye on soil alkalinity by using a simple pH soil-testing kit if you are using mains water with a high level of lime – some plants will tolerate an alkaline soil, others will soon suffer. Use clean rain-water from a covered storage tank for acid-loving plants, but do not be tempted to use water from a domestic water softener.

Feeding

Plants, like any other living things have a requirement for food. While green plants have the ability to make sugar in their leaves during photosynthesis, they rely on their roots to take up certain essential minerals from the growing medium; having said that, the leaves are also able to take up small amounts of dissolved mineral. These plant foods need to be replaced from time to time to compensate for those used by the plant and others lost by leaching due to heavy rain, or by irrigation with excessive amounts of water. But care should be taken to prevent damaging levels building up in the soil which would scorch roots and, as far as nitrogen is concerned, be washed out into the waterways.

Animal manure was used as the main source of plant food until some hundred years ago. This was dug directly into the soil and, later, certain manures such as cow manure were suspended in sacking material in a vessel of water to make 'cow tea'. Since then, chemical manufacturers have made up compounds from inorganic sources, and the science is much more precise.

Common name   none
Botanical name   *Escallonia* 'Donard Brilliance'
Hardiness rating   Slightly tender
Care rating   Fairly easy
Description   Evergreen and grows well at the seaside. 6ft (1.8m)
Peak interest   Summer
Growth rate   Fast
Soil needs   Any well-drained soil and will tolerate lime; sun or partial shade
Treatment   Thin out and cut back straggly shoots mid-summer
Propagation   2–4in (50–100mm) long cuttings in summer

However, we are now in an environmentally sensitive age and the use of synthetic materials is being questioned. Whether a fertilizer is organic or inorganic matters little to the plant because soil bacteria convert both to the same chemical which enables it to be taken up by the roots. But there is a difference in price: the organics such as hoof and horn or bonemeal are usually more expensive than the equivalent inorganic chemical.

Plants require different types of fertilizer in varying amounts. The greatest need for many plants, including young vigorous shrubs, is for nitrogen to encourage leaf growth. Phosphate is used for good root development and maturity; potash to promote steady, healthy growth, flower and

Common name   Golden Bell Bush
Botanical name   *Forsythia* 'Lynwood'
Hardiness rating   Hardy
Care rating   Easy
Description   Deciduous shrub with upright growth. 6ft (1.8m)
Peak interest   Spring
Growth rate   Fast
Soil needs   Any well-drained soil in sun or semi-shade
Treatment   Thin out congested growth when flowers fade
Propagation   4–6in (100–150mm) long cuttings mid-summer; 8–10in (200–250mm) long cuttings late autumn

fruit production. There may be an added need for certain other elements such as magnesium and calcium to be given from time to time, but the necessary traces of boron, zinc, manganese, molybdenum and some others are normally present in sufficient quantities in most types of soil. There is a need for these to be added to loamless media at the outset, and from time to time with long-established plants growing continuously in the same medium.

Fertilizers can be quick acting to stimulate growth and these include synthetic urea and sulphate of ammonia. Epsom salts is a quick-acting form of magnesium, so essential for healthy green leaves. These fertilizers are useful as a tonic to remedy deficiencies and to boost growth. Other

fertilizers, such as urea formaldehyde, are available which give up their nutrients gradually over a longer period.

Slow-acting fertilizers are ideal for mixing with container media to replace organic feeds such as hoof and horn which can be less stable, especially when a large proportion of fine dusty particles is present in the fertilizer. They are often recommended for use as a base dressing to incorporate into the soil before planting the shrub. While 'straight' fertilizers can be mixed at home, it is usually more convenient to use compounds blended by the manufacturer. These are available at retail gardening outlets and the container lists recommendations for various uses. Most fertilizers are used for general feeding but some have a special use, for example aluminium sulphate which is used to enhance the blue flower colour of hydrangeas.

Foliar feeding is often recommended, particularly if a plant is affected by disease, or some other root disorder. An extremely alkaline soil or, in some cases, a very acid soil can restrict the uptake of some elements and so it may be necessary to resort to foliar feeding for that reason. Soluble fertilizers such as urea or nitrate of ammonia provide nitrogen, mono-ammonium phosphate contains phosphate as well as nitrogen, and potassium nitrate gives potash in addition to nitrogen. Even greater care than that applied to root feeding should be taken when applying foliar feeds, because the leaves can be easily scorched by an overdose, or when application is made in bright sunlight.

Liquid feeding is a convenient way to provide plants with nutriment, especially those growing in a container when they may be fed at the same time as watering. Diluters are available to attach to watering equipment. These monitor the correct amount of soluble fertilizer to mix with irrigation water as it passes through, but do ensure that no back syphoning occurs when the system is linked to the public water mains. It is, in fact, illegal to attach such a device to the mains without suitable equipment.

Timing of fertilizer application is important. There is little use in providing the plant with food when it is in a dormant state. Autumn application of nitrogenous fertilizers should be avoided to prevent soft, lush growth which would be prone to frost damage. Spring is a good time to apply fertilizer, with another application during early summer. Fertilizer should always be applied when the soil is moist. This is particularly important for plants growing in containers, especially when liquid feeding, to avoid root scorch.

Special fertilizer compounds for shrubs are available from garden centres and other retailers. Full instructions for use will be found on the container label.

Mulching

Organic matter is one of the main constituents of healthy productive soil. Bulky organics such as garden compost or farmyard manure can be effectively dug into the ground before planting, but when plants like shrubs remain in the same position for more than a few months, some other method needs to be employed to ensure that the humus content remains satisfactory. Mulching provides the answer, and the idea is to spread a layer of material over the soil surface so that worms can drag the fragments down to lower levels over a period of time. The actual time taken for the mulch to find its way into the ground depends on many factors including the acidity or alkalinity of the soil, which in itself has a bearing on the number and types of worms present.

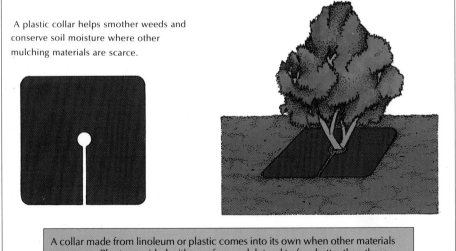

A plastic collar helps smother weeds and conserve soil moisture where other mulching materials are scarce.

A collar made from linoleum or plastic comes into its own when other materials are scarce. Plants provided with a surface mulch tend to fare better than those without: the soil is generally warmer, especially when the mulch is of a dark colour; soil moisture is conserved during periods of dryness, and weed growth is suppressed. Mulching prevents a cap of crusty soil occurring after heavy rain; mulches of a bulky organic nature often provide a bonus in the form of plant foods.

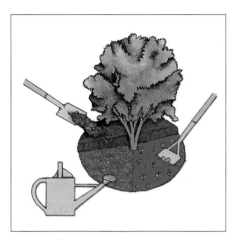

Good mulching practice. Having hoed off weeds and loosened the surface soil, apply a top-dressing feed and water it well in. Finally spread a layer of mulching material over the soil.

Aesthetically, a mulch improves the appearance of the garden, it reduces the need to weed, it suppresses moss and lichen, and helps to retain soil moisture in periods of drought; it keeps the soil warmer and yet at the same time evens out the extremes of temperature, keeping roots cooler in summer. A bulky organic material, with the aid of earthworms and bacteria, adds humus to the soil. One important factor is that a mulch will prevent rain splashing soil up on to the leaves and, at the same time, prevent a hard 'pan' forming on the soil surface. It will prevent clay from cracking, make the soil more congenial and reduce leaching of nitrogen and other nutrients.

There are plenty of materials available for use as mulches, including pebbles which were once used by the Romans and are now favoured by landscapers. Pebbles in various colours and different sizes can be purchased from garden centres. Gravel can also look attractive in the right setting, such as below dwarf shrubs on the rock garden. Peat has been used in the past but is now considered by some to be anti-conservational. It is being replaced by processed tree bark which is available in various grades, from very small chip, ideal for small shrubs, to medium grades for general woodland-type subjects such as camellias and azaleas; the coarse chips are more suited to large plants, for example rhododendrons. This grade, incidentally, can also be used for surfacing paths. Coir (coconut fibre), once used in Victorian times, is available again. The finer grades of all of these products are very attractive to birds who enjoy scratching about in the material to hunt for insects. To keep adjoining areas tidy, lay a narrow width of netting down over the mulch along the border to prevent spillage on to the lawn or path. There is a possibility that galvanized netting may rust and then release excessive levels of zinc which would be toxic to plants. The alternative is plastic-covered netting, the brown colour being inconspicuous.

A comparatively new product consists of wood chips baked at high temperature and then 'mineralized' to reduce rotting. The chips are then dyed with various colours, including green, redwood and brown. Light colours may be used to brighten up a shady spot, or colours may be mixed to create a subtle mosaic in the garden to complement the shrubs.

Sawdust and other organic materials lacking in plant foods can be used, provided they do not contain toxic substances, for instance excessive levels of tannin, or turpenes. However, it is important that they are supplemented with added nitrogen when they are put into position. This should prevent bacteria depleting the soil reserve as they break down the material, which would lead to deficiency within the plant. Spent mushroom compost is useful under certain conditions; it tends to be rather alkaline and contains comparatively high levels of plant nutrients, since mushrooms do not take up the same kinds of element as green plants. Spent hop 'manure' is useful when available and does not contain an excessive amount of unwanted plant nutrient.

Farmyard manure, well rotted and free from debris and weed roots is sometimes used around shrubs. Its fertilizer content is somewhat unpredictable and it is inclined to introduce unwanted weed seeds. Composted lawn clippings, mixed with other material in the compost heap, make a good mulch; thick wads of lawn clippings alone, however, should be avoided because they are inclined to pack down into a slimy mass.

Treated sewage sludge in various forms is available in some areas; before use, however, it should be checked for levels of zinc and other trace-element chemicals which may be toxic. Leaf mould makes a good, natural mulch but do be on the lookout for a possible hazard in the form of Boot-lace fungus, often called Honey fungus (*Armillaria* spp.) due to its smell and the colour of the fruiting bodies. This plant disease grows on the roots and below the bark and rind of plants; it sends out strands similar in appearance to bootlaces and can easily be collected along with leaf mould. Once in the garden, it is virtually impossible to eradicate.

Manufactured sheeting such as black polythene is available with perforations, small enough to allow the passage of air and water, but too small to allow light through to encourage weeds to germinate and grow. This kind of sheeting can be camouflaged by covering with a thin layer of soil, so that it will be inconspicuous and yet serve the purpose of a mulch. Polythene sheeting should not, however, be used to cover badly drained soils, otherwise it may encourage stagnation. Plants themselves can also be used as a mulch, particularly low-growing subjects such as *Cornus canadensis*.

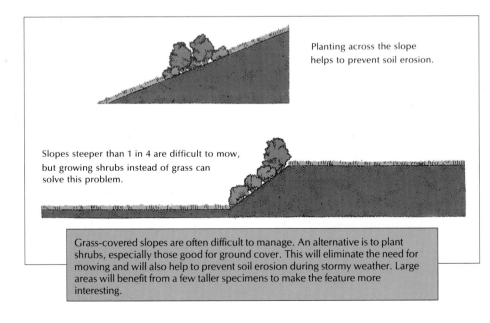

Planting across the slope helps to prevent soil erosion.

Slopes steeper than 1 in 4 are difficult to mow, but growing shrubs instead of grass can solve this problem.

Grass-covered slopes are often difficult to manage. An alternative is to plant shrubs, especially those good for ground cover. This will eliminate the need for mowing and will also help to prevent soil erosion during stormy weather. Large areas will benefit from a few taller specimens to make the feature more interesting.

Mulches are best applied when the soil is moist, otherwise some plants, especially those which have a shallow root system, may suffer as a result of dryness before the rain is able to filter through the mulch. However, if the soil is too wet, the mulch may prevent evaporation, and if it is very cold it may take a long time to warm up. Spring is the best time to put down the mulch. Avoid placing the material over established weeds which should first be hoed off. Care should also be taken to prevent the mulch, especially those based on manure or garden compost, from touching the plant stems.

Pruning

Many gardeners find the act of pruning difficult but there is no real reason why they should, provided the simple rules are kept in mind. In the first place, it should be established whether or not the shrub needs pruning at all and so it is worth considering the main reasons for cutting into the plant. Dead or badly diseased wood should be removed; damaged stems and branches need to be cut out before they die back; old

When sawing off larger branches, always undercut a quarter way through from the underside before cutting down from above. This helps to prevent the branch splitting.

and spent branches should be removed to make room for new, more vigorous stems. Generally, the centre of a bush should be kept sparse to allow sunlight to penetrate and to ensure good air movement. The removal of weak shoots helps to avoid congestion; unwanted suckers growing

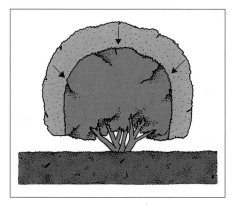

Heading back reduces the shrub size by up to a third.

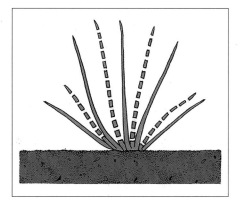

Selective thinning. Cut out unwanted wood leaving healthy productive growth.

Root pruning.

from below ground, particularly those growing from a rootstock should be removed – although they should, strictly, be pulled away from the root rather than cut off, which would only encourage further sucker growth. Also, the plant often needs to be encouraged to keep looking tidy and to stop it from encroaching upon its neighbours. Evergreens are often lightly pruned at planting time to reduce transpiration and thereby reduce the strain on roots.

Hard pruning, i.e. removing long lengths of stem, especially in winter, tends to encourage more vigour. Cutting into the current season's growth during late summer often reduces vigour. Unfortunately all shrubs cannot be pruned at the same time in the same way. Pruning before flowering will reduce the amount of blossom. The majority of plants should be pruned just after the flowers fade. This will give sufficient time for the plant to recover and make way for new, healthy and vigorous growth which will flower when the time comes. Pruning can be an unpleasant

task during frosty weather; in any case, the plant is susceptible to bark splitting and disease when pruned under those conditions.

Pruning Group 1 (PG1)

These are plants that flower in winter and spring, or early summer on growth made last year; they should be cut back after flowering, to within two or three growth buds of the older framework. This gives room for new shoots to grow and it may be necessary to remove some of them to allow the sun and air to ripen the remainder.

Pruning Group 2 (PG2)

Plants flowering on last year's and the current year's growth in spring and summer are, again, pruned after flowers have faded. This time, start by cutting away last year's spent wood, then if it is necessary, to allow more light and air, cut back the weaker growth.

Pruning Group 3 (PG3)

In general, plants which flower in the late summer/autumn on wood made during the current season are pruned in late winter after the risk of severe frost has passed. This will give new shoots the opportunity to develop and mature in time for the next flowering period.

Pruning Group 4 (PG4)

These are the shrubs that produce flowers during the summer, but are grown primarily for their brightly coloured bark. They are cut back hard in spring, to within two or three growth buds of the old framework.

Certain subjects, such as Prunus triloba, flowering in early spring, produce blossom on stems made during the previous year. In order to encourage the plant to produce flowers again next year, cut back the spent wood immediately after flowers fade to within two or three buds of the older wood (see PG1, page 38). The resulting new stems are then retained as replacements to produce next spring's blossom.

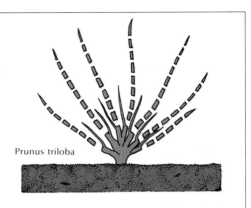

Prunus triloba

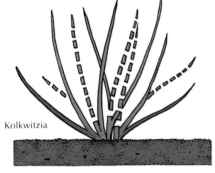

Kolkwitzia

Some plants, for example Kolkwitzia, flower in spring on growth made the previous year, but also on older wood. In this case, approximately one quarter to one third of the old wood should be removed after the flowers fade (see PG2, page 38). The plant should remain reasonably vigorous and healthy with this method, the complete bush being refurnished with younger stems every three to four years.

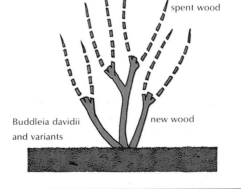

spent wood

Buddleia davidii and variants

new wood

Shrubs, such as Buddleia davidii, which produce flowers on the current season's growth in late summer and autumn, are pruned in late winter by cutting back the spent wood to within two buds of the main framework (see PG3, page 38). Vigorous, tall-growing subjects prone to wind-rock in autumn can be made less susceptible by reducing the length of their stems soon after the flowers fade.

Pruning Group 5 (PG5)

This group is easiest of all, consisting of those plants with, normally, tidy growth but which do on occasion produce the odd 'rogue' shoot that needs to be trimmed.

Pruning Group 6 (PG6)

This final group includes those shrubs that withstand clipping with shears – evergreens in late spring and late summer, deciduous kinds from summer to early winter.

Use only tools with a sharp blade for the job of pruning; jagged edges and bruised tissue allow disease spores to enter the wound. So-called wound-healing paints should be avoided because they are inclined to seal disease spores in the wound; far better to ensure the cut is made with a smooth surface and just above a growth bud so that it heals quickly. The wood of different species varies in density: one plant may be easily cut with secateurs, while a shrub with a similar-diameter stem may require loppers; a Grecian pruning saw may even be necessary for another.

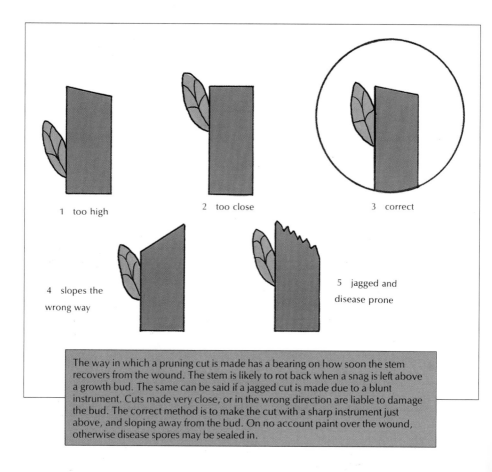

1   too high

2   too close

3   correct

4   slopes the wrong way

5   jagged and disease prone

The way in which a pruning cut is made has a bearing on how soon the stem recovers from the wound. The stem is likely to rot back when a snag is left above a growth bud. The same can be said if a jagged cut is made due to a blunt instrument. Cuts made very close, or in the wrong direction are liable to damage the bud. The correct method is to make the cut with a sharp instrument just above, and sloping away from the bud. On no account paint over the wound, otherwise disease spores may be sealed in.

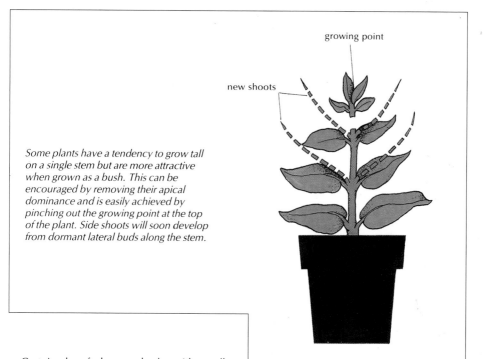

growing point

new shoots

Some plants have a tendency to grow tall on a single stem but are more attractive when grown as a bush. This can be encouraged by removing their apical dominance and is easily achieved by pinching out the growing point at the top of the plant. Side shoots will soon develop from dormant lateral buds along the stem.

Certain dwarf clumpy shrubs with small leaves, such as erica, can be clipped with shears, but large-leaved shrubs should always be cut with pruners. The important thing to remember is to select the right tool for the job, which really means a tool that will sever the stem without too much effort and strain. Needless to say, the tool should be kept sharp, cleaned after use and kept free from rust by wiping over with an oily rag. Moving parts should be lightly oiled to reduce wear.

Weed Control

While many people find hand weeding enjoyable and relaxing, others would prefer to resort to other methods of eradication. There are different kinds of hoe that will sever weeds but some shrubs are surface rooting and great care should be taken to avoid dislodging or, even worse, chopping through the shrub roots. The aim of hoeing is to cut through the weed stem just below soil level, then rake the weeds off before they have a chance to root.

Mulching has already been discussed and that method is, no doubt, the most worthwhile provided the material is deep enough to suppress the weeds. Some chemicals are manufactured for weed control around shrubs. They need to be chosen with great care, because the chemical is just as likely to kill the shrub as the target weed. Read the instructions on the container carefully, having made sure that the herbicide can be used around shrubs — the majority cannot.

3 • PROPAGATION

Shrubs can be increased by the use of various methods of propagation. These include seed, cuttings, layering, suckers and grafting. Given the correct environmental conditions, each of the methods will provide good results but one is usually preferable than another for a particular species. Some gardeners appear to have 'green fingers' but success really amounts to providing the correct temperature, moisture, relative humidity, oxygen, and for leafy plants, carbon dioxide and light of the correct intensity and duration. The medium in which the propagant is placed, must be free from pests, diseases, toxins and excessive levels of fertilizer. It is also important to propagate from pest and disease-free stock, otherwise the problem will also be increased.

Sow very small seed by sprinkling it evenly over the surface. Space it well out. A folded piece of paper facilitates sowing. Then press the seeds gently into the surface of the medium.

Seed

Many shrubs can be raised from seed but home-saved seed from hybrids, or closely related plants which have been cross-pollinated are unlikely to produce offspring the same as the parent. Purchased seed is relatively inexpensive and many plants can be raised at the same time. While the seed from some plants germinates quickly, other kinds can take a year or more. In all cases, it usually takes much longer for a plant grown from seed to reach maturity, compared with one grown from a cutting.

Some seeds, especially those within a fleshy fruit, are best stratified. This consists of storing seeds in cool, moist conditions in the presence of air. One well-tried method is to place the seed in alternate layers with sharp sand, or peat and sand mixture in pots or boxes which are buried six inches (150mm) deep in well-drained soil. The container contents will then undergo low temperatures during winter. A period of from between two to eighteen months may be necessary according to species.

Seeds with hard seed coats sometimes need coaxing by soaking them in water overnight, preferably in a warm place, or chipping the seed coat; treating with boiling water or alternate freezing and thawing sometimes works well.

The seed of certain species can be sown in open ground out of doors provided it is well drained. Most seed, however, is sown in containers. These could be small flowerpots or pans, or when a large number of seeds need to be sown, seed trays come into their own; a very good compromise is to use half pots of the kind dwarf chrysanthemums are grown in. The type of growing medium used should suit the types of plant being grown, remembering that some plants require an acid medium, whereas others require an alkaline sort; the vast majority of seedlings require a medium approaching neutral. Seed-sowing medium can either be based on loam, in which case properly made John Innes seed compost usually gives good results. It consists of

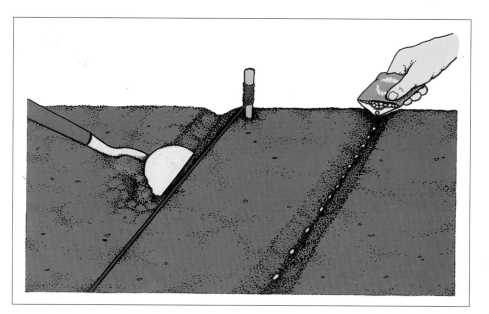

Sowing seeds in a drill.

loam, peat, coarse sand, superphosphate and ground limestone. Many loamless kinds of media are also available: pure sphagnum peat, a mixture of peat and sand, horticultural vermiculite or Perlite; coir (coconut fibre) and processed bark are often used. Ready-mixed proprietary products are available utilizing these materials and only require water to start them off.

The way to prepare the container (which should be clean and dry) is to fill it with the medium, then give the base a sharp tap on a hard surface. The top is then struck off level with a straight edge. Lightly firm the medium – the base of another flower pot could be used for the purpose – then sow the seed thinly and well spaced out. Fine seed should be simply pressed into the surface, but larger seed is usually covered with the medium to a depth of twice the diameter of the seed. Containers with large seed can be watered with a fine rose, but others will need to be placed in a vessel of water until the surface is moist. In fact, the same method can be used for containers

Pricking out. Prick out seedlings as soon as they are large enough to be handled: small plants yet to develop their first true leaves establish much faster than larger seedlings. Hold them by their seed leaves as the stem and true leaves (if present) are delicate and will bruise easily.

sown with larger seed to avoid disturbance. All that remains is to cover the container with a sheet of glass and exclude light with newspaper. The container is then placed preferably in a cold frame, or an area where birds and mice are unlikely to cause problems.

Once the seedlings have emerged, the glass and paper should be removed, but take precautions against damage by low temperature, or strong sun. When large enough to handle, the seedlings are pricked out into containers containing John Innes No. 1, or loamless medium.

Vegetative Propagation

The alternative to raising plants from seed is to increase them by vegetative methods.

One of the advantages of this is that the plants come true to type. However, there are some disadvantages in that there is a possibility of carry-over of pests and diseases present on the host plant; sophisticated facilities are often required and while some plant material can be stored for short periods, leafy cuttings in general are more difficult to store and transport than seeds.

Certain plants, such as *Kerria japonica*, that produce suckers can be reproduced by division. This can be carried out during the dormant season when the soil is not frozen or too wet. The method is to dig up the plant and then split the roots, each portion containing the stems intact. The portions are then replanted separately.

Non-suckering plants and those which are difficult to root by other means may be layered. This involves wounding the stem,

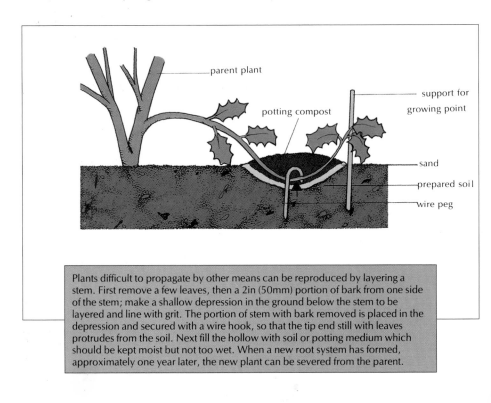

parent plant

support for growing point

potting compost

sand

prepared soil

wire peg

Plants difficult to propagate by other means can be reproduced by layering a stem. First remove a few leaves, then a 2in (50mm) portion of bark from one side of the stem; make a shallow depression in the ground below the stem to be layered and line with grit. The portion of stem with bark removed is placed in the depression and secured with a wire hook, so that the tip end still with leaves protrudes from the soil. Next fill the hollow with soil or potting medium which should be kept moist but not too wet. When a new root system has formed, approximately one year later, the new plant can be severed from the parent.

either by removing a strip of rind, or by cutting into the stem with a sharp knife. The wounded portion of stem is then buried while still attached to the host; the apex end of the stem protruding from the ground is tied to a cane vertically. Roots eventually grow from the wounded area and after approximately one year, the rooted portion is cut from the host and then replanted.

The majority of shrubs can be success-fully increased by cuttings, although this method can present a challenge, because there are variables, such as the time of year and the type of cutting that is likely to root successfully. For example, there are soft cuttings which are taken from new stems; semi-hardwood cuttings which are stems with a firm base, produced during the current growing season; then there are hardwood cuttings which consist of a firm stem throughout.

Soft cuttings are taken from lateral shoots and are approximately 3in (75mm) to 5in

Common name   Tree Hollyhock
Botanical name   *Hibiscus syriacus* 'Woodbridge'
Hardiness rating   Slightly tender
Care rating   Fairly easy
Description   Erect deciduous shrub with bushy habit. 6ft (1.8m)
Peak interest   Summer
Growth rate   Fairly fast
Soil needs   Any well-drained soil in full sun
Treatment   Cut back any straggly growth in early spring
Propagation   Cuttings 2–4in (50–100mm) long late summer

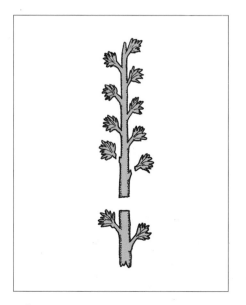

Soft stem cuttings.

(125mm) in length. The cutting is severed from the host and cut across just below a node. Remove the lower leaves, leaving those from half-way up to function properly. Dip the base of the cutting into hormone rooting powder and then insert into rooting medium. A propagator with misting unit and soil warming cables is the ideal, although many cuttings will root well when the container is placed in a polythene bag to form a tent. When growth appears to be taking place, roots can often be seen just protruding through the holes of the container. When the cuttings are furnished with roots they are potted off singly into individual containers, or may be hardened off in a cold frame before planting in the open later.

The technique for semi-hardwood cuttings is much the same as for soft cuttings, except that they are taken during summer when the base of the stem has slightly matured and become firm. One method that has been used in the past for subjects difficult to root is carefully to tear the lateral shoot forming the cutting from its host. This results in removing a small portion of the parent's stem in the form of a 'heel'; the heel is then shortened to approximately ¼in (6mm) long and inserted in the same way as a soft cutting.

Hardwood cuttings are made from the current season's wood that has matured. Late autumn/early winter is usually a good time to take the cuttings. They can be 6–12in (150–300mm) long according to species, after removing any immature stem at the top; the cut at the top should be back to just above a growth bud, and below a node at the base. Use a hormone powder relevant to hardwood cuttings, then insert the cuttings to at least half their depth in well-drained soil outside, or in containers in a cold frame. Evergreen shrubs can be propagated in the same way as that described for deciduous, except that they are normally rather shorter and need protection from drying, cold winds.

Some species do not perform well on their own roots for one reason or another; there are others which cannot be rooted from cuttings. These problems can be overcome by grafting a small portion of one plant on to a rootstock of another of the

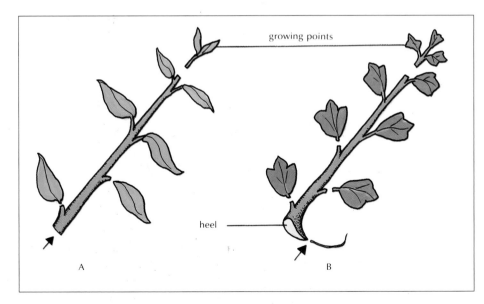

Semi-ripe cuttings. Remove the lower leaves and the growing point. Cut the lower end of a nodal cutting (A) just below a leaf joint. With a heel cutting (B) neaten off stringy bits of bark attached to the heel.

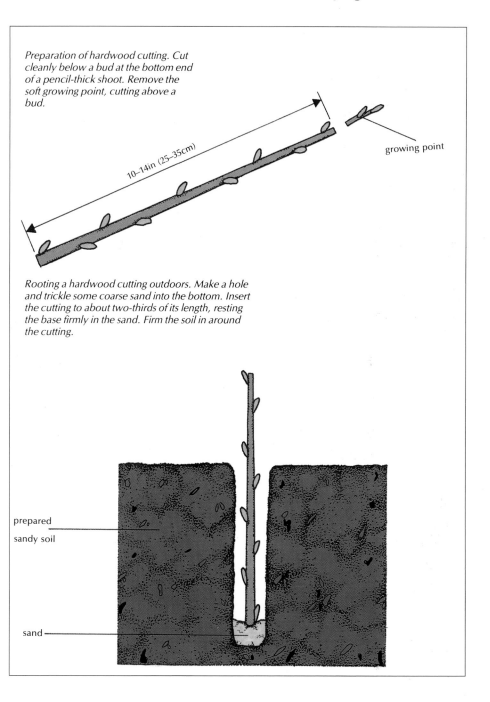

Preparation of hardwood cutting. Cut cleanly below a bud at the bottom end of a pencil-thick shoot. Remove the soft growing point, cutting above a bud.

10–14in (25–35cm)

growing point

Rooting a hardwood cutting outdoors. Make a hole and trickle some coarse sand into the bottom. Insert the cutting to about two-thirds of its length, resting the base firmly in the sand. Firm the soil in around the cutting.

prepared
sandy soil

sand

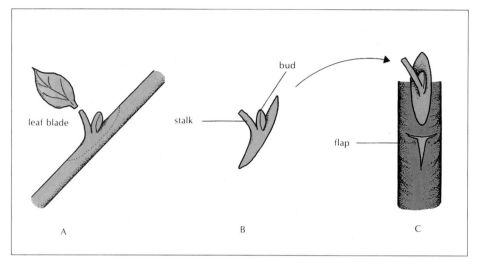

leaf blade

stalk

bud

flap

A

B

C

Budding.

Deciduous azaleas are a blaze of colour during spring.

same species. For example, roses are grafted, usually by taking a growth bud together with a small shield-shaped section of outer stem and placing it behind the rind of a rootstock stem. This form of grafting is known as 'budding'. Another form of grafting involves taking a small portion of woody stem, as if preparing a hardwood cutting, and placing that in the rootstock plant.

There are three points to watch out for when grafting. Firstly, that the rootstock and the scion variety are compatible; secondly, that the polarity of the scion is correct, that is, it must be the right way up; and lastly, that the contact between the two cambium layers must be close and secure.

Experiment with different methods of propagation and keep a diary of dates with the kind of rooting medium used, type of cutting, etc., temperature, if any, and of course, the name of the plant. It can be a fascinating hobby, and financially rewarding, too.

4 • AILMENTS

In listing different pests, diseases and disorders, it might appear that shrubs are difficult to grow and subject to a lot of problems. That is not so, provided they are growing in suitable surroundings and treated with reasonable consideration. The majority of plants remain healthy throughout their life but, in keeping with other living organisms, they may be attacked by parasites from time to time and so it is advisable to be aware of the symptoms. Sometimes these symptoms are masked so that diagnosis needs some detective work as, for example, when the leaves are wilting. This may simply be due to dryness at the root, or alternatively it could be caused by root disease.

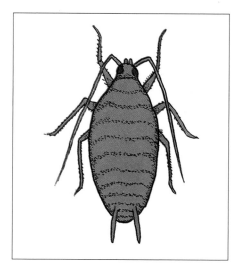

Aphid.

Pests

Ants

Ants are a nuisance because they tunnel around roots and dislodge them, and they swarm over plants searching for aphids for the honeydew they secrete. Ants also take certain aphid species below ground and encourage root-infestation. The pests can be caught in jars filled with sweet liquid such as sugar water, or narrow greasebands can be placed around the stems of plants, but that method is somewhat difficult in the case of multi-stem shrubs. Pouring boiling water over the nest entrance has also been effective, but take care not to damage the plant roots.

Aphids

Aphids, often called Greenfly or Plant lice, suck sap and cause distorted leaves and stems. The honeydew they secrete attracts sooty mould, which in itself is harmless, but looks unsightly. Aphids can be dislodged from the plant by using a forceful spray of clear water, or the colony may be rubbed off with the finger. If it is necessary to use a pesticide, use one that is specific to aphids only so that it will not harm beneficial insects.

Caterpillars

Various caterpillars large and small chew foliage from time to time. Certain kinds, such as the Rose leaf-rolling sawfly larva, spend their life protected by a rolled leaf. Some gardeners may be happy for their shrubs to be hosts, while others look upon these visitors as pests. In that case, the larvae are easily dealt with by hand-picking. On a large scale, they may need to be controlled by using an insecticidal spray.

Chafer Beetles

Chafer beetles of one kind or another attack shrubs. The Cockchafer, often known as the May bug, lays eggs in the soil from which hatch thick, fleshy and dirty-white grubs. These larvae feed on the roots of

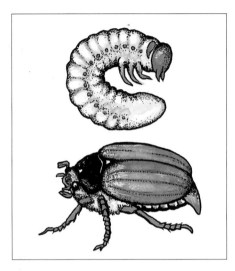

Cockchafer beetle and larva.

plants. The Garden Chafer is somewhat smaller than the Cockchafer. The adults eat holes in leaves; their larvae attack roots and can do a considerable amount of damage to young plants. The third Chafer to look out for is the Rose Chafer. It is a larger beetle than the Garden Chafer and has a metallic, bright golden-green colour. Again, the larvae feed on roots. The best way to trap the larvae is to place upturned turves around plants so that the pest can be collected up when they congregate below the sod. Naphthalene is distasteful to the grubs and is often effective when applied to the soil in late spring or autumn and watered in.

Cuckoo Spit Insects

Cuckoo spit insect derives its common name from the frothy bubbles secreted by the larvae of the Frog-hopper. The larvae suck the sap and cause the leaves and tender shoots to wilt and become deformed. The larvae can be removed by hand or, better still, forcibly washed off with a strong jet of water to remove the 'spittle' and insect.

Leafhoppers

Leafhoppers lay eggs below the skin of leaves and the resulting larvae suck sap, causing mottling and premature leaf fall. Control is difficult, other than by using an insecticide which should be sprayed underneath the leaves and over the ground below.

Leaf-Miners

Leaf-miners are larvae of small moths or flies which tunnel in the leaf between the upper and lower skins, eating the contents as they go to leave characteristic 'mines'. The pest can easily be squashed between finger and thumb nail, but in the case of a large infestation, it may be necessary to resort to insecticidal spraying; in this case, the ground below the shrub should be sprayed as well, since the larvae often pupate in the soil.

Mealy Bugs

Mealy bugs are closely related to Scale insects; they differ in that the adults are mobile and they are covered by a white, waxy excretion. The colonies feed on sap by puncturing the rind which sometimes allows the entry of disease spores. Forceful applications of clear water are sometimes an effective control, or methylated spirit can be used; otherwise it is a case of using an insecticide.

Scale Insects

Scale insects resemble miniature tortoises, approximately ¼in (6mm) in diameter, or less according to species; others are in the shape of a small mussel shell — hence their common name of Mussel scale. They are mobile only in the juvenile stage but all stages reduce the vigour of the plant by sucking its sap. They secrete honeydew in the same way as aphids, attracting ants and wasps. Inspect any new shrub acquisitions carefully for this pest, because once established it can multiply into large colonies very quickly. Scrape the pest off with a finger nail, or use a seed label. Methylated spirit on the end of an artist's brush can also be effective when the insect is lifting its shell to reproduce in spring.

Slugs and Snails

Slugs and snails are among the best known of all invaders of plants. They attack seedlings by chewing leaves, and eating soft stems. The pests often attack at night and can easily be seen with the aid of a torch and dealt with accordingly. Various traps like upturned grapefruit skins are effective, shallow containers of stale beer have also been known to attract, and drown them.

Weevils

Weevils can be very destructive, especially the adults during late spring and summer, when they chew holes in leaves. They are particularly difficult to catch by hand because they fall to the ground as soon as they detect movement. However, they can be caught in traps of rolled corrugated paper, sacking, or a piece of board placed below the target shrub.

Diseases and Other Problems

Bud Drop

Bud drop is often caused by mischievous birds, especially in spring when the buds are beginning to break. Unfortunately, those methods which are usually successful in deterring birds are often unsightly and the shrub border is hardly the place for them. These include silver paper, or other reflective material such as a mirror suspended from the plant. Cotton threaded through the plant is sometimes effective. Bird repellents in the form of sprays are unlikely to be effective unless they have a gritty texture.

Another form of bud drop is caused by a lack of moisture at the roots, especially during the short period before bud-break.

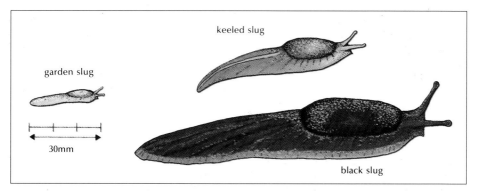

keeled slug

garden slug

30mm

black slug

Slugs can be a real problem for many gardeners.

Canker

Canker affects the stem and shows as a sunken lesion, often cracked with raised corky tissue surrounding the infection. The problem often arises when two branches have rubbed together, or when a snag has been left at pruning time. Prevent damage to the bark whenever possible, avoid painting over wounds, but do make them smooth with a sharp blade or rasp. When canker is present, it should be cut out, preferably by removing the branch back to an area where there is no longer any internal staining.

Chlorosis

Chlorosis usually occurs when the plant is deficient of a certain plant food. Yellow leaves at the base of the plant, particularly when the veins remain green, suggest that it is lacking magnesium, possibly due to the fact that it is growing in chalky soil. Magnesium sulphate (Epsom salts) is the answer here. Yellow leaves and stunted growth can also result from a lack of nitrogen. Yellow leaves at the stem apex are more likely to indicate a deficiency of iron or manganese. In all cases, fertilizers should be applied according to the instructions on the container label.

Coral Spot

Coral spot is a disease which can infect living tissue as well as dead. It produces pinkish pustules and is readily seen. The best way to prevent this problem is to avoid leaving snags when pruning, and to collect up all prunings and other woody material lying about the garden.

Damping Off

Damping off disease affects seedlings, causing them to topple over at soil level. The majority of these water-borne pathogens are introduced by watering from containers where the water has been stored without a cover. Infection can also come from using dirty pots and seed trays, and by using once-used, or 'unclean' sowing and potting media.

Die-Back

Die-back can be caused by a true parasite, or it can be physiological, or mechanical. In any event, it is where the shoot dies back from the tip. Cut away the affected part back to a healthy growth bud without leaving a snag, avoid painting the wound and transplant the subject to a more favourable position if the problem is an annual occurrence due to frost.

Leaf Spot

Leaf spot is the result of attack by a variety of diseases. Each spot is caused by a single spore alighting on the leaf and then sending out minute feeding tubes. The majority of leaf spots occur during damp weather and apart from correct pruning technique to allow air and sunshine to penetrate the plant, protective fungicidal spray may be used.

Mildew

Mildew usually shows as a whitish covering on leaves, stems and/or buds; there are forms which produce a brownish covering similar to velvet. These symptoms should not be confused with the natural characteristics of some plants which produce similar features. Plants infected by mildew lack vigour, their leaves are often distorted and fall prematurely. The best way to prevent mildew is to avoid any check to growth by proper feeding, watering and general care. The only

Common name   Camellia
Botanical name   *Camellia japonica*
Hardiness rating   Hardy
Care rating   Easy
Description   Evergreen with glossy green leaves. 6–10ft (2–3m)
Peak interest   Spring
Growth rate   Medium
Soil needs   Acid well-drained in semi-shade
Treatment   Avoid dryness at roots to prevent bud drop
Propagation   Cuttings 3–4in (75–100mm) long in summer

way to control the disease already infecting a plant is to spray with a fungicide.

Rust

Rust appears on leaves and stems as brown- or orange-coloured pustules. The disease is becoming more widespread in certain plants, especially roses. Although pruning is sometimes effective, more often than not a fungicide needs to be used. Fallen leaves should always be collected up.

Wilting

Wilting foliage can be caused by dryness at the root, wind, strong sun after a spell of dull weather, waterlogging, frost thawing too quickly, canker girdling the stem, incorrect use of pesticide, overfeeding, or root disease. Of these, the last is likely to create the most difficulty in correcting. Honey fungus, often known as Bootlace fungus (*Armillaria* spp.), attacks a wide range of plants by penetrating the tissue of the roots by means of growths resembling bootlaces. Plants wilt and eventually die due to this disease because it is difficult to apply a fungicide sufficiently concentrated to eradicate the fungus without seriously affecting the host. However, some people believe that they have saved plants by using phenolic applications and there is at least one proprietary product available with a label recommendation. If a plant is showing symptoms of attack, carefully lift some bark from the stem at ground level. If cotton-like threads of mycelium can be seen below, the chances are that Armillaria is present, especially if a honey-like smell can be detected. Sometimes yellow toadstools appear close to infected plants but that is not always the case.

When Armillaria disease is confirmed, it would be advisable to remove the plant, together with surrounding soil so that adjacent plants do not become infected. The bootlaces, correctly called rhizomorphs, can travel a considerable distance in the soil to find a new host.

Although the majority of woody plants are prone to the disease, some, especially privet, are more susceptible than others. Herbaceous plants also need watching because they are not immune and some vegetables like potatoes have been known to suffer. The best safeguard is to keep your plants healthy and vigorous by proper feeding and watering; initial selection is also important so that as far as possible, the appropriate subject is planted to meet the requirements of soil, site and aspect.

5 • PLANT A – Z

The following list consists of plants that are reasonably easy to grow and should flourish in a wide range of soils provided the ground has good drainage.

Aesculus parviflora (Dwarf Buckeye)
A broad dome-shaped shrub producing suckers from below ground. White flowers in summer, followed by fruit when the summer is warm. Remove dead wood in winter or early spring. 10ft (3m)

Berberis x *stenophylla*
Graceful weeping stems with thorns produce yellow flowers in spring followed by berries in summer. Thin out old wood in spring. 6ft (2m)

Buddleia alternifolia
Lilac-coloured flowers are produced by pendulous stems in summer. Cut out old, spent shoots after flowering. 20ft (6m)

Cornus florida (Flowering Dogwood)
Showy white flower heads in summer; the leaves turn bright red in autumn. Cut out congested wood after flowering. 15ft (4.5m)

Cotinus coggygria (Smoke bush)
Maroon-red leaves provide an attractive backdrop for flower heads that resemble puffs of smoke. Excellent autumn colour. 6–10ft (2–3m)

Cornus *(Dogwood) prefers alkaline soils and a sunny site.*

Cotinus coggygria *'Royal Purple' is an outstanding foliage shrub.*

Daphne retusa
Slow-growing evergreen producing fragrant, pale rose-pink flowers in summer, followed by berries in autumn. 3ft (1m)

Erica carnea 'Springwood White'
Semi-prostrate shrub good for ground cover. Considered to be the best winter-flowering heath. Clip to remove two-thirds of previous year's growth after flowering. 1ft (300mm).

Fatsia japonica
Evergreen producing large, glossy leaves. White flowers in winter. An excellent plant for a container on the patio. Cut back straggly growth to the base in late spring. 10ft (3m) in open ground.

Fothergilla major
Fragrant flowers in spring are followed by leaves which produce bright tints in autumn. Remove straggly shoots after flowering. 8ft (2.4m)

Fuchsia 'Riccartonii'
A hardy plant good as a specimen or to form a hedge. Red/purple flowers are produced

over a long period in summer. Cut damaged and congested stems back to ground level in spring. 6ft (2m)

Hebe 'Autumn Glory'
Evergreen with glossy, greenish-purple leaves. Violet-coloured flowers throughout summer. Trim if necessary in spring. 1½ft (450mm)

Kalmia latifolia (Calico Bush)
Evergreen with glossy-green leaves. The white or pink flowers, in late spring, resemble cake icing. Cut back any straggly stems after flowering in late spring. 6ft (2m)

Magnolia soulangiana *with its bold, goblet-like flowers is one of gardening's gems. It makes a first-class specimen shrub.*

Kalmia latifolia *'Clementine Churchill' is first class on acid soils, provided it is sheltered from cold winds.*

Kerria japonica 'Pleniflora' (Batchelor's Buttons)
Vigorous shrub with glossy-green stems. The double yellow flowers appear in spring. Suckering tends to be invasive. Remove spent stems after flowering, and the tips of others that have died back. 6ft (3m)

Leycesteria formosa (Flowering Nutmeg) (Pheasant Berry)
Vivid green stems are erect and hollow. Small flowers backed by bright-red bracts

appear in summer, followed by deep-red fruit in autumn. Prune away old wood in spring. 6ft (2m)

Magnolia soulangiana
Pink-tinged, white flowers appear in spring before the leaves. Tolerates polluted air and makes an attractive focal point in the lawn. No pruning necessary. 12ft (4m)

Osmanthus delavayi
Slow-growing, rounded evergreen with fragrant, white flowers in spring. Trim to shape after flowering. 9ft (2.7m)

Pachysandra terminalis
Excellent evergreen for use as a ground-cover plant. White flowers are produced in spring. Pruning not necessary, other than removing leafless stems occasionally. 6in (150mm)

Philadelphus 'Virginal'
A vigorous shrub producing double or semi-double, fragrant white flowers in spring. Prune spent stems close to main framework after flowering. 10ft (3m)

Phlomis fruticosa (Jerusalem Sage)
Evergreen with silvery, grey-green stems and leaves. Yellow flowers in spring. Thin out congested growth and cut back old, spent stems in spring. 3ft (1m)

Pieris japonica *is an excellent foliage shrub.*

Pieris 'Forest Flame'
Evergreen producing bright red new growth in spring, the growth turning pink, then white to green. Small white flowers appear in spring. Trim after flowering if stems become straggly. 6ft (2m)

Potentilla fruticosa (Shrubby Cinquefoil)
Dense growth useful to suppress weeds. Yellow to orange flowers in summer. Avoid hard pruning – buds will not grow from old wood. 3ft (1m)

Prunus laurocerasus 'Otto Luyken'
Compact evergreen with a spreading habit good for ground cover. It produces white flowers in spring followed by purple-black berries in autumn. Trim straggly stems after flowering. 4ft (1.2m)

Pyracantha rogersiana 'Flava' (Firethorn)
Evergreen shrub with thorny stems. White flowers in spring followed by yellow berries. Little pruning necessary unless an odd shoot straggles, which should be cut out in spring after flowering. 6ft (2m)

Ribes sanguineum (Flowering Currant)
Vigorous shrub with pink flowers in spring. The cut stems are good for forcing indoors, but the resulting flowers are often white. Remove congested growth after flowering. 8ft (2.4m)

Rosmarinus officinalis (Rosemary)
Dense evergreen with aromatic foliage. The purple flowers appear in spring, followed by flushes later. Trim to shape after first flush of flowers in spring. 6ft (2m)

Senecio 'Sunshine'
Once known as *S. laxifolius*, or *S. Greyi*, this evergreen produces leaves with a silver underside attractive for floral arrangements. Yellow flowers appear in summer. Shorten stems in spring. 4ft (1.2m)

Spiraea bumalda 'Anthony Waterer'
Variegated leaves with flashes of white and pink make this an attractive plant; the pinkish-coloured flowers are a bonus in summer. 2½ft (0.75m)

Viburnum tinus (Laurustinus)
Evergreen producing fragrant flowers from late autumn through winter, followed by berries in summer. 10ft (3m)

Weigela florida
Deciduous shrub with attractive spreading stems. Red flowers appear in summer. Remove congested growth by cutting back spent stems after flowering. There is also a variegated-leaf form which provides added attraction during the growing season. 10ft (3m)

Pyracantha *'Orange Glow' is a large evergreen, well suited for use as wall cover. The bright red berries develop in autumn and persist well into winter.*

Senecio 'Sunshine' has interesting foliage and yellow daisy-like flowers from June to August.

Spiraea is both a flowering and a foliage shrub. Its carmine flowers, borne in clusters from July to September, glow against its golden green leaves.

Plants for Special Soils

Clay

Berberis	Rosmarinus
Cornus	Ribes
Cotoneaster	Rosa
Forsythia	Spiraea
Kerria	Vinca
Philadelphus	Weigela
Pyracantha	

Peaty

Azalea	Hamamelis
Calluna	Magnolia
Camellia	Mahonia
Chimonanthus	Pieris
Daphne	Pernettya
Erica	Rhododendron

Chalky

Cotoneaster	Ribes
Deutzia	Spiraea
Forsythia	Syringa
Hypericum	Viburnum
Philadelphus	

Dry Sandy

Berberis	Lavendula
Cytisus	Potentilla
Erica carnea	Senecio
Genista	Spiraea
Hebe	Vinca
Hypericum	

Damp Site

Aronia	Salix caprea
Calycanthus floridus	Sambucus
Clethra	Sorbaria
Cornus stolonifera	Spiraea x veitchii
Photinia villosa	Vaccinium
Prunus spinosa	Viburnum opulus

6 • SEASONAL GUIDE

Growth phases in plants are governed by a number of different factors, including site, aspect, soil type, latitude and cultural details such as pruning, feeding and irrigation. One year can be very different from another in the timing of seasons: an early spring can start off well, only to be followed by a cold spell ending with the possibility of frost during early summer in some locations. Therefore, the detail given here may well vary when compared with particular situations. It can only be a guide and is intended to prompt the memory so that the various jobs can be planned ahead.

Spring

With any luck, the worst of the weather will now be over and so shrubs should be inspected for winter damage; shoots showing signs of frost damage and die-back, plus those broken by the weight of snow or wind should be cut back to healthy buds. In any case, many subjects that flower on the current season's wood should now be pruned, together with those grown primarily for their decorative bark. Towards the end of the period, early spring-flowering shrubs will also need to be pruned.

Much depends on the weather as far as rose pruning is concerned: large-flowered hybrid tea bushes are often pruned during early winter in favoured areas, while rose-growing enthusiasts in other areas cut the stems only one-third back at that time to avoid wind-rock, leaving the main pruning until spring. Either way, the bushes should now be pruned by cutting out unwanted growth completely and the stronger shoots back to half length. Cluster-flowered floribundas can also be pruned during spring.

Shrubs that are not normally pruned but that have already produced flowers which have faded should be dead-headed, taking care not to damage any buds that are just below the spent flower cluster.

Common name   Oregon Grape
Botanical name   *Mahonia* 'Apollo'
Hardiness rating   Hardy
Care rating   Easy
Description   Evergreen with fragrant flowers. 4½ft (1.4m)
Peak interest   Flowers winter; berries summer
Growth rate   Medium
Soil needs   Any well-drained soil in shade or semi-shade
Treatment   Cut back if necessary after flowering
Propagation   Lift rooted suckers in late autumn

Seeds that have been stratified over winter can now be sown in a nursery bed, or in containers. When the seed is being sown in the ground, it is better to remove any weeds present and then to sow the seed in straight drills to facilitate weeding later on.

The planting of bare-root subjects should be completed before the sap begins to rise and leaf buds begin to break. Remember to protect evergreens from cold wind as soon as they are planted. Ensure newly planted shrubs are kept moist at the root, then apply a surface mulch.

Be on guard against frost and spray blossom over with clear water before the sun reaches them; camellia flowers are particularly vulnerable to early-morning sun after frost.

Watch out for the rapid build-up of pests like aphids, as they multiply rapidly at this time of year. If there are any particular diseases, such as mildew, that regularly attack certain plants each year, you may wish to give them a protective treatment with a fungicide.

Now is a good time to apply fertilizer to the shrub border.

Summer

Keep newly planted shrubs watered during dry periods. The majority of plants that produce blooms on the previous year's growth will have finished flowering by the end of the period and so congested, spent wood should be cut out to make way for new shoots. Others that have started to flower will be encouraged to extend their flowering period by deadheading the faded blooms. It is essential to keep spring-flowering shrubs moist at the root now to enable them to begin to initiate next year's flower buds.

Although any time is good to visit other people's gardens, summer is particularly worth while to get new ideas. Many gardens are open to the public at this time and a number have a plant stall which often provides the opportunity to purchase an unusual, or even rare, plant.

Keep on top of weeds, otherwise they will compete with the shrubs for plant food, soil moisture, and in some cases light and air. Weeds are also inclined to attract pests.

Mid-summer is a good time to take soft cuttings of shrubs: the stems are at an ideal stage of growth and environmental conditions are conducive to rooting. The stems will be firm towards the end of summer so that semi-ripe cuttings can be taken from many subjects.

Viburnum davidii *provides evergreen ground cover on chalky soils in light shade, or can be used for hedging.*

With daylight hours getting shorter towards autumn, late summer is the time to ensure everything is up-together in the shrub border, especially if there are many demands on time and only evenings and week-ends are available for gardening. It is advisable to take advantage of favourable soil conditions to make planting positions ready for bare-root evergreens ordered during the growing season.

Autumn

Evergreens and, later on, bare-root deciduous plants recently purchased may be heeled in if it is necessary to delay planting for a day or two: it is essential to prevent the roots from drying out. Check on supplies of fertilizer and bulky organic materials so that planting can go ahead

Rhododendron yakushimanum *needs acid soil and semi-shade but is a very fine specimen shrub.*

without interruption. There is every chance that there will be a sharp frost at any time and so tender shrubs growing in containers should be given protection. The frost tends to loosen soil around the roots of recently planted subjects and so firming may be necessary.

Autumn is a good time to take hardwood cuttings for insertion into well-drained soil. A sprinkling of grit at the base of the cutting will help to prevent rotting before the cuttings have had a chance to make roots. The cuttings can often be made from stems that have been pruned. Tall-growing shrubs like *Buddleia davidii* should be half-pruned before autumn gales rock the plants. This is done by shortening the current season's

growth by half, to be followed next spring with the usual cutting back to two or three buds from the main framework.

This is a good time to visit gardens open to the public to see autumn leaf colour and make a note of interesting plants, provided frost or high wind has not spoilt the effect.

Winter

The end of the calendar year but not the end of the gardening year for that is a continuous cycle: the end of the year for one plant is midway for another and the beginning for others. A good example of the way in which plant seasons can be mixed is when shoots of spring-flowering shrubs such as flowering-currant, forsythia, *Jasminum nudiflorum* and mahonia when cut now and brought indoors will produce their flowers that much sooner. Placed in a container of water in a warm room during midwinter, they may even be in flower for Christmas.

Buds developing on shrubs in the border may require protection from birds; rabbits can also be a problem at this time in country districts. Snow may cause damage if a heavy fall remains on the branches. Shake the snow from branches so that the weight will not break the stems and spoil the look of the plant; the resulting wounds would allow disease spores to enter the wood.

Continue planting and transplanting when soil conditions permit. Stems layered, and hardwood cuttings taken a year ago may be sufficiently rooted to transplant now. Plants delivered from the nursery will possibly be wrapped in straw. This can remain on the plants for a week if necessary, but do take off any polythene that has been attached so that air can move around the plant. Better still, plant the new acquisition as soon as it is delivered.

The turn of the year will see days lengthening, so every opportunity should be taken to catch up on any outstanding work.

Forsythia *is very tolerant of a wide range of soils and can be relied upon to produce a good show of blossom in early spring.*

GLOSSARY

Acid (soil) Having a pH below 7.
Acuminate Having a gradually tapered point.
Acute A leaf with a sharp point.
Adventitious A growth or organ present where it would not normally be, e.g. roots growing from a stem.
Alkaline (soil) Having a pH above 7.
Apex The tip of a stem, leaf, or petal.
Axil The angle formed between leafstalk and stem.
Axillary A shoot arising from an axil.

Ball The formation of roots in a container.
Berry A fruit whose seeds are enclosed within a pulpy or juicy substance within a skin.
Bloom (Bloomy) A fine powdery-like waxy deposit.
Bottom heat Artificial heat applied to the base of a propagator.
Bract A leaf-like organ or a degenerate leaf immediately below a flower.

Calcareous Containing chalk or lime.
Calcifuge A lime-hating plant.
Calciphilous A lime-loving plant.
Coir Processed coconut fibre.
Composite A plant belonging to the daisy family (Compositae).
Compost (1) A mixture of loam, sand and cocofibre or other ingredients to make a potting medium for plants.
Compost (2) Decomposed vegetable material rotted down to incorporate into the soil.
Cultivar Garden variety of plant, or form found in the wild and maintained as a clone in cultivation.
Cutting A portion of root, stem or leaf of a plant used for propagation.

Damping overhead Sprinkling with water to freshen foliage.
Deciduous A plant which loses its leaves each autumn.
Dibber A cylindrical tool usually made from wood or plastic which is used to make planting holes for seedlings.
Dioecious Male and female flowers on different plants.
Distichous Leaves arranged oppositely, and superimposed in two ranks.

Evergreen Remaining green during winter.
Exfoliating Peeling off in thin strips.

Fastigiate Erect growth.
Fertilizer Chemical providing plant food.
Florets Small, individual flowers within a dense inflorescence.

Grafting Joining one part of a plant to another so that the pieces unite to form one plant.

Habit Manner of growth.
Harden off To acclimatize plants gradually to cooler conditions.
Hybrid A plant grown from seed resulting from a cross between two distinct species or genera.

Inflorescence The flowering part of the plant.
Internode Portion of stem between two nodes.

Lanceolate Shaped like a lance-head.
Lateral A shoot, stem or bud arising from another.

Monoecious Male and female flowers separate, but on the same plant.
Mucronate The short, stiff point of a leaf.

Node The place on the stem, usually swollen, bearing bud or leaf, the 'joint'.

Pan (1) The surface crust on soil formed after heavy rain.
Pan (2) A solid layer of mineral below soil level.

Pan (3) A container used for plant propagation.

Peat Partially decomposed vegetation, usually acidic and varying in colour from pale yellow to black according to the source.

pH A scale that measures acidity or alkalinity. pH7 is neutral, below pH7 is acid, above pH7 is alkaline.

Prick-out To transplant seedlings.

Processed bark Shredded and milled tree bark which has undergone processing by composting to remove harmful agencies like turpenes and tannin.

Propagation To raise a plant by sowing seed, or vegetatively by taking a cutting, by grafting, or by division.

Semi-evergreen Normally evergreen but losing some or all of its leaves during winter.

Shrub A woody plant which branches from the base with no obvious trunk.

Standard A trunk without lateral stems below the head.

Sucker A stem produced from below ground level.

Trunk The clear portion of stem below the head.

Watering in To apply water around newly planted roots.

Kolkwitzia amabilis *(Beauty Bush)*.

INDEX